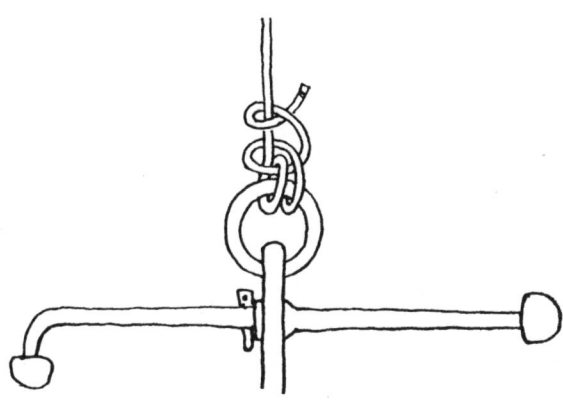

SEA-BOATS, OARS AND SAILS

by
CONOR O'BRIEN

with thirteen pages of drawings by the author,
photographs by Tim Cooke,
and design drawings by François Vivier

With a Foreword by SAM LLEWELLYN

Lodestar Books

First published 1941 by Oxford University Press
This edition published 2013 by
Lodestar Books
71 Boveney Road, London, SE23 3NL, United Kingdom

www.lodestarbooks.com

A CIP catalogue record for this book
is available from the British Library

ISBN 978-1-907206-17-7

Typeset by Lodestar Books in Equity

Printed in Spain by Graphy Cems, Navarra

All papers used by Lodestar Books
are sourced responsibly

CONTENTS

LIST OF ILLUSTRATIONS

(at end of book)

FOREWORD

THERE ARE MANY THINGS TO RECOMMEND the owning of small boats. The principal advantage, of course, is the power it confers to row away from the land until there is enough wind to fill a sail, and to return to a universe that would have been immediately recognizable to our swamp-dwelling ancestors. The other advantages are less obvious but equally seductive. There is the frenzied espousal of a particular philosophy of seagoing—to engine or not to engine, to camp or to cabin, to socialise or to make like a hermit. There is the settling on the precise boat that will fulfil that philosophy—a process with most of the joy and none of the pain of falling in love, since adored objects that you build yourself don't talk back or run off with the plumber. Late at night before sleep drowns you there is the half-dozing analysis of every land, rivet and gadget. And last but not least, there are the multifarious dodges and wheezes of seamanship.

The endearing thing about Conor O'Brien (a man, come to think of it, who might not have been pleased to be called endearing) is that he is just as much a victim of his sea dreams as anyone who is likely to shell out for this book. He comes on like a pundit; the running order is strictly logical, starting with the raw materials of boatbuilding and ending with dodges and wrinkles of seamanship. It is an ancient format, and in the hands of less interesting writers can reduce the reader to unconsciousness as fast as an express train behind the ear. Because O'Brien shares his readers' obsessions, he carries us along with him, even if only to argue with him. He is a fervent advocate of home building in carvel, a method most home boatbuilders will find about as easy and attractive as DIY root canal work. He powerfully advocates the building of a canvas canoe or curragh, and maybe he has a point. He deplores gaff rig and sliding gunter. Some of his stuff is very good—look, for instance, at his remarks on hypotenuse mooring and tying up in a rock gully subject to a six-foot swell (where has he been?). Some of the stuff he recommends he hasn't even tried; but, hey, he admits as much, and it's not going to stop him. So let's try it ourselves, eh?

Someone will probably object that this is a book written some time ago, and will question its relevance to the modern age. They will be barking up the wrong tree. Books about refitting the headlining to your carbon-fibre fifty-footer in its marina berth are obsolete by the time they are written. I mean fashions in colour-ways change so fast, darling, and the evolution of foam-backed vinyl is *continuous*. The truth is this: books about the joy of building and sailing simple but perfect boats, like the François Vivier design that illustrates these pages, can never stale. Cruising small boats under sail and oar is always (weather permitting) a delight. And when the weather is horrible and the boat is in the garage, thinking about sailing them is another.

Sam Llewellyn
November 2013

Publisher's Note

We are grateful to boatbuilder and sailor Tim Cooke for permission to reproduce his photographs of *An Suire (The Sea-Nymph)*, the beautiful clinker-ply lugger he built to François Vivier's ILUR design, and which he sails in waters off south-west Ireland which were familiar to Conor O'Brien; and to François Vivier for permission to reproduce his design drawings on pages 174-5.

Conor O'Brien makes reference to the same page of his own drawings from various parts of the book, so we have followed the organisation of the 1941 edition by placing all his drawings at the back, where they are most easily located when required.

We have not improved on the perfunctory index of the first edition, however the book is not a very long one, and familiarity with it will soon be acquired.

The reader will have no difficulty solving the mystery described on page 62.

I

INTRODUCTORY

BOATS ARE OF INNUMERABLE TYPES, varying with their use and the waters they are used in, but within its own sphere each type of working boat is fixed. Not so with pleasure boats; their design changes at the caprice of fashions which follow racing practice, vaguely and often unintelligently, and each change increases their cost and their preciosity. These are times for realism, and nothing needs debunking more than the yachting and boating business. There are now many people, and there will be more, who would like to own sailing boats but are deterred by the supposed expense of the game and the suspicion that owners are not, after all, getting sea-value for that expense. But if they ask for a plain boat with no frills on they are shown some venerable relic with misfit sails and prehistoric gear, and they are warned off craft which may be entirely efficient and up-to-date, but do not conform with the latest fashion, by the horrible threat of being branded as unorthodox. Most of what is written about boats is naturally based on the orthodox view, and the man who wants a boat neither for class racing nor as a harbour ornament, but to go to sea in, gets little guidance from it. This book of mine is frankly unorthodox, in that I hold nothing sacred and take nothing for granted. I do not puff my wares with graphs and formulae like a quack medicine; if the reader does not accept my conclusions by the light of his own common sense let him reject them; I am no pontiff, merely a seeker after truth.

By a sea-boat I understand one that is a means of transport as well as something to go sailing in; one that will bring her owner to whatever place he wishes on any day when boats of the same size are out fishing. It may be as good to journey hopefully as to arrive, but a journey with not even the idea of arriving anywhere is apt to be boring; I at least have always enjoyed most those cruises which had a definite object. The boat must be fit for the journey in every way. The rules of the sea put safety first, and safety is best assured by simplicity of gear; the completion of the passage depends on speed, and speed is mainly a matter of size; the arrival in port must not be made anxious by qualms about a bad landing, as it will be if the boat is very costly and fragile. I must stress the matter of size, because the increasing cost of yachts and boats has reduced their size till they are only fit for the finest conditions and so slow that long passages are a penance or an impossibility.

In writing this book I have been guided entirely by considerations of practical utility, though I have not forgotten the old saying that no ugly ship was ever a good one, and I have tried out in practice most of the suggestions here made, before committing them to print. Chapters II-V show various boats as they are likely to be seen by a prospective purchaser, their construction, qualities, and the features I approve or disapprove of. Chapter II may be a deterrent to the amateur builder, but as there is more satisfaction in a thing made with one's own hands than in one merely bought, and as some special types of boats, like the one described in Chapter VI, cannot be bought, and a home-made job, however crude, is better for very special work than a misfit, I give what I think is the easiest method of building, with workshop details. Other conditions, for instance, carriage on the roof of a car to exposed fishing water, difficult beach work, or frequent portages, require a combination of lightness and seaworthiness which is best exemplified in the curragh of the West of Ireland; that also cannot be bought, and as it is easy to build I give directions for doing so. Chapters VIII-XI overhaul all the equipment which may or may not be in a boat when bought or which may be bad and need alteration or replacement, and suggest some gadgets and fancy rigs for those with experimental minds. The last four chapters are on the handling of boats and general seamanship. Really bad conditions at sea are often passed over as things that do not happen to the amateur boatman; but he may be called upon at any time to save life. That call overrides all considerations of safety first, but if it finds him unprepared he may be an added danger to the man in distress. Our small boats cannot do much in the way of rescue work, but I have put together from instructions for larger boats what I think we might do, hoping that my readers may be able to amplify from other sources what I have written.

A book of 220 pages[1] cannot cover the whole subject of boats. I have omitted many details of seamanship whose descriptions are easily accessible elsewhere or which are better learned from a study of the actual work. I have omitted the pram, whose construction is obvious, and whose virtues of lightness and cheapness are offset by her vicious behaviour under oars; also the dory, and all other craft with

---

1   As laid out in the first edition — Ed

flat bottoms or angular bilges, for though cheap they cannot be light, as their form is inherently weaker than a round bottom, and it is also less sea-kindly, however well it may suit a speed-boat. I make no mention of full-powered craft, and I do not think an engine as auxiliary to sail is justified in a boat of the size I have in mind—not more than 25 feet in length and a ton in weight. I have not considered the question of racing at all. Class races are won on the windward leg, and go to boats of fabulous cost and limited utility for other work, but handicap races can be won by any boat which, though she may not be a star performer to windward, can keep up a high speed on a reach. This she will best achieve not with cast-off racing sails and gear, but with the rig suitable for her type, with sails well-cut and well cared for, properly stretched and set and accurately sheeted, and her hull trimmed truly to its marks. As races are often lost through slovenly sail-trimming, so they may be won by close attention to the smallest change in the force or direction of the wind, so that every inch of canvas is pulling its hardest all the time. With the rigs and with the gear which I advocate in the following pages, with a good helmsman and a smart crew, I claim that the sea-boat could, in her own weather, put up a very creditable fight against the more costly but less seaworthy craft which a mixed race gathers to oppose her.

II

CONSTRUCTION AND MATERIALS

HIS IS NOT A TREATISE ON BOAT-BUILDING, about which there are
several complete and excellent books, but merely a short description of the
construction of a boat, which may help a buyer to secure a sound craft and to do
repairs to her, and save him from weakening her by injudicious alterations. And it
is a convenient place for a glossary of the various parts of her.[1] The names of these
are not the same in all districts, so my definitions must be accepted throughout
this book.

Most boats are built on a keel, to which the frames, or transverse ribs, are
fastened. It is deep enough to be an important source of longitudinal stiffness in
such craft as yachts, which have a considerable rise of floor—that is, where the
frames rise steeply from their connexion with the keel. In this case the garboards,
or the lowest strakes of planking, are nailed to a rabbet cut in the keel near its top.
But in small boats which have a flat floor it would be very wasteful to cut such a
rabbet at the correct angle, so the keel is left square in section, and a wider strip
of wood called a hog-stave[2] is fastened above it to nail the garboards to. The boat
could in fact be completed without a keel, and some types do not have any. Since
the floor planking, the relatively flat part of the skin below the sharp curve at the
bilge where it turns up to form the nearly vertical topside, provides plenty of lateral stiffening, the keel of an ordinary boat is not made very wide—two inches
is a likely figure—but it is made deeper, whether or no it is needed for stiffening
against vertical bending strains, in order to keep the planking off the stones when
grounding on a beach.

At either end of the keel the stem and stern-post are fitted, generally halved to
it; but sometimes the stem is merely butted on it, which is just as good, because
there is no strength in this joint, anyway, and the halving leaves a longitudinal
crack into which sand and stones may be forced when the boat is being hauled up;

---

1   They will also be found named on Fig. 1.
2   Often called the kelson; but properly the kelson is the longitudinal piece lying above the
    frames, seldom used in boat construction.

and sometimes the stern-post is tenoned into the keel, which is definitely better, as then the joint cannot touch the ground. The strength of these joints is obtained by stem and stern knees or deadwoods, substantial crooks of oak somewhat wider—or, as the builder would say, with more siding—than the keel, which cover and are bolted to the keel and the stem and the stern-post respectively. The rabbet in the keel, or the bevel on the hog-stave, if the keel is not rabbeted, is continued up the stem and stern knees and across the stern-post up to the height of the tuck, that part of the stern-post clear below the transom.[1] It is customary not to cut a rabbet on the stem for the ends of the planks, but to nail them to a wider piece of wood called an apron-piece fastened inside it, as the hog-stave is on the keel. This assemblage of parts is now set up vertically on the stocks, and carefully shored up to keep it so.

From this point there are two different ways of carrying on the work. You may fit the permanent frames either sawn out of curved pieces of wood or steamed and bent to the shapes previously determined by the drawings, but in any case pretty rigid, and build up the skin on them; or, as is more usual in this country, you may shape the skin on temporary moulds, and when it is complete and fastened together all over, bend lighter frames inside it. The former method is suited to carvel build, in which the plank edges are merely butted and not fastened together, for the only fastenings are in the frames, and the skin cannot exist without them, while the clench-built boat, in which the planks are fastened together by their overlapping edges, can go to sea with hardly any frames at all. I have seen a seventeen-foot Norwegian boat with only three frames—excluding two little cant frames[2] in the bow and stern which were hardly more than breast-hooks.[3] But the practice in this country is to space the frames 9 inches or so apart at most.

A carvel boat, unless built with very thick planks, must be closer framed or the planks would spring apart in the spaces between, and it is much more laborious to make the frames beforehand than to bend them in last of all, so that build is not popular. It makes a better job, however, in several ways. If it is adopted for a small

---

1   Transom has two meanings: 1, the flat board forming a square stern, as here; 2, the thwart-ships beam supporting a counter, as in Chapter VII.

2   All ordinary frames are set at right-angles to the keel; cant frames are raked, in this case they were fastened to the stem and stern knees and raked towards midships.

3   Breast-hooks: horizontal angle-pieces connecting gunwales and stringers to stem.

light boat we do not try to cut all the frames that are needed from grown crooks of oak—the grain is not likely to run true enough for them to be strong without being inordinately heavy—but we bend them inside ribbands—light strips of wood fastened to temporary moulds as the planks of a clench-built boat are. When they are secured to the gunwales and stringers the moulds and ribbands are taken away and the planking proceeded with on the frames

Formerly it was a common practice to notch the backs of the frames so as to fit the laps of clench planking. I have seen a boat, said to be more than a hundred years old, with incredibly thin elm frames so treated. But it is a tedious and difficult job—the frames have to be steamed and bent into place, and then taken out again and notched—and more of a weakness to them than a strength to the planks, unless these are very wide and thick.

The width of plank that may be used depends on the section of the hull. Norwegian boats, which have a great rise of floor and a great flare—the projection of the gunwale beyond the water-line—giving them a wide V section, have very wide planks; the seventeen-foot boat I have mentioned has only four a-side; the *dorna* of Arosa Bay in Spain is equally crude, though it has more of a round at the bilge. To work round the curve of the boat's bottom the top edge of the lower plank has to be bevelled on the outside for the next plank to lie fair over it, and if it is bevelled too severely there's nothing left to hold the nails. If the bevelling is skimped the plank is likely to split down the middle when it is nailed tight, unless, of course, it is planed hollow on the inside; so in boats of the usual British section narrow planks are used to work round the bilges and only a small bevel is cut on each. It is not possible to use very wide planks in a flat floor, as they have to be cut with a heavy sny, or curve on the edge; and it is undesirable to use very wide ones in the topsides. The lands, or projecting edges of the planks, are conspicuous, and it looks bad to have them of irregular widths.

In carvel planking the strakes about the bilge must be even narrower, for they are not helped round the curve by bevelling, but the whole plank is bent transversely; it is therefore more liable to split and has a tendency to curl out at the edges. But as the seams are invisible they may run any way that economy in cutting the plank suggests. A boat has two or three times as much girth amidships as at the ends, and it is an obvious economy to get over the excess by putting in one or more short lengths of plank there; the use of such pieces, tapered at both ends, called stealers, is quite legitimate and saves cutting some of the heavy sny that is needed in a clench-built job.

The ends of carvel planking fit on to the stem or transom without any more work than cutting them the right length, but with clench planking the bevel changes to a short square rabbet working out to a feather edge so that they lie flat on whatever they are nailed to. Don't cut off the after-ends of the planks, which make a convenient handle to hold them by, till all the fastenings are in, when they may be trimmed flush with the transom.

In clench work the edges of the planks are fastened together with one or two rows of nails between the frames, riveted over roves, or copper washers. In carvel work the nails pass through the frames, two to each plank, but they need not be roved, if the frames are of oak, elm, or ash. A copper nail turned over to form a hook and well clenched holds just as well in hard wood. Nailing the plank-ends to the stem and transom needs some care in selecting the right size of nails and the right bit to make holes for them; but once the plank is well home there is not enough strain to draw a square copper nail out of oak or elm; you are likely to do more damage by bending the nail and splitting the plank if the hole is too small. When in doubt jag the corners of the nail with a chisel before driving it. It is more difficult to keep the seam between the garboard strake and keel or hog-stave tight, especially if the boat has a centreboard; if she leaks there, put in some nails long enough to clench through the hog-stave. Even in soft wood holes must be bored for copper nails. A small drill makes a better hole than a bradawl. You can buy the machine at Woolworth's, and a knitting-needle makes a better bit than a twist drill, which is too brittle and gets choked with the fragments of wood. Flatten the end of the needle in the fire, don't harden it too much, and grind it to a drill point rather sharper than you would use for metal work.

The garboard strake is the most difficult one to put on, for it has a heavy wind in one or both ends; amidships it lies almost horizontal, but it has to be twisted to lie on the vertical stem and stern-posts. Fitting it to the stern-post seems to me needless labour and risk of breaking it, moreover, it leaves narrow pockets between the plank and deadwood in which dirt and water lodge. The boat's performance is not seriously prejudiced if the garboard is carried on up to the transom, leaving the tuck of the stern-post and the deadwood naked, instead of being twisted down to cover them. Of course it would spoil a vessel with a big rise of floor and a long narrow run, but such a type is outside the scope of a book about boats.

It is unwise to try to fit a garboard strake cold; forcing the end into a nearly right-angle twist is likely to break off the upper forward corner of it or to pull it away from the keel amidships; the end should be softened with hot water, which is swabbed on while it is held over a fire and given the appropriate twist by hand— don't burn your hand; clamp a bit of stick to the end to hold it by. If you want a garboard strake with a twist in each end it is better to make it in two lengths scarfed together amidships. Fit both ends and clamp them in place, and then bring the cut parts together and mark the scarf; remove them, cut the scarf, and then put them back and fasten them, working amidships from both ends; don't nail the scarf till all the rest of the plank is fastened. Scarfs may be used elsewhere to save wasteful cutting of planks which would have a great deal of sny, but should be well staggered, and should not be used in the way of the bilges. All scarfs are made with the outer points facing aft; their faying surfaces, like all joints used in boat work, should be rubbed with thick paint before nailing. Copper tacks, clenched but not roved, will hold them tight. A spile-hole is bored in the garboard to drain the boat. If it is ⅞-in. in diameter the ordinary cork will fit it. If the garboard is soft wood nail a hard-wood patch on outside and make the hole through that, and it will not be torn by contact with stones.

We may suppose that the skin of a clench-built boat is now complete, kept in shape partly by the three moulds to which it is lightly nailed, but mainly by its own curved form. If it is of pine or other soft wood it has no great strength, for the only fastenings are rows of nails some ⅜-in. in from the edges of the planks, which could easily be split off. The light steamed frames are put in to guard against this splitting rather than to give rigidity. Except for one or two right forward, each is in one piece, its centre nailed down to the keel. The steaming is easy. You do not want a regular steam-box, which is rather a difficult thing to find the materials for, if you can get a length of wide iron pipe. Plug one end of it, put that on the ground and prop the other up at an angle of forty-five degrees or so. Fill one-third with water, and build a fire round the lower end. Insert your timbers, and plug the upper end lightly—you don't want to shoot the plug through someone's window or blow your breech-block out. The time taken for steaming timbers depends on their thickness and the closeness of the grain of the wood; they should be quite soft and flexible when taken out—with an old pair of gloves, for they must be pressed into place at once before they cool.

The place for the frame is marked by a double pencil line inside the planking. Midway between the lines the planks are bored, and a copper nail entered in each hole from outside. The hot timber is now bent down inside the boat by pressing on its centre enough for one end to be clamped to the top strake at the proper spot; don't press the centre any more, or you may break it, but go to the other end, and push that down, forcing the bight hard against the planking. When it is as tight as it will go, and lying accurately between the pencil lines, clamp the second end, and drive the nails up through the frame; they will go through the hot wet wood without wanting holes to be bored if you hold a weight against the frame, or, if the boat is too big for you to reach, have someone else inside her to hold it. Don't rove or clench the nails till the wood has dried and hardened.

The next item is the gunwale. Spaces must be cut in the corners of the moulds to allow this to be fitted, which is done in various ways. The most usual is to cut down the heads of the frames to the depth of the gunwale below the top of the sheer-strake, and fasten the gunwale to that only, which is all right if the sheer-strake is a good piece of hard wood. But gunwales get plenty of knocks and strains, and these are liable to split the strake. A better plan, but a laborious one, is to notch the heads of the frames half-way into the gunwale, so that they help to support it. I prefer to carry the frames right up to the top of the strake, and run a lighter gunwale[1] clear inside them, the only fastenings being through all those; it is not so rigid as a gunwale fastened to the strake, but for that reason less likely to get broken. It is usual to cover the gunwale and the top of the strake with a thin flat capping, which is a nuisance to put on and is easily torn off. In a small boat much used on beaches I should certainly omit it, and put the gunwale inside the frames; that looks untidy, but it is practical, because you can turn the boat upside down and wash all the sand and mud out of her through the spaces between the frames. In that case those spaces must be filled up in the way of the breast-hook

---

1   More properly inwale.

and quarter-knees, which connect the gunwales with the stem and transom re-spectively, and also in the way of the clamps for the rowlocks.

Struts are now put across the gunwales to keep them apart while the moulds are removed to allow the risings to be put in. These are stringers running the length of the boat to support the thwarts, though fastened inside the frames; they add little to the constructional strength. Bilge stringers may be similarly fitted, to hold the floorboards down; they have not much other value, and short cleats hold the boards just as well.

The thwarts are a vital part of a small boat, in which the keel is not an im-portant structural member. The resistance to longitudinal bending of any vessel, except one with straight and upright sides like a barge, depends on her sides being kept at the same distance apart. Without the thrust of the thwarts to do this, her ends, which have less buoyancy in comparison to their weight than her mid-body, tend to drop and her sides to close in; she loses her sheer, the upward sweep of the gunwales at bow and stern, and becomes in sailor's parlance 'hogged'. Sag-ging down amidships is not so common a condition, but it may happen to a lightly built boat if she lies on a beach with no support amidships, or is hoisted out of the water by her two ends, so the thwarts should be effectively fastened to her sides to prevent them from spreading.

This is a summary description of the building of a common boat, and if it is not detailed enough to be of much use to the amateur builder, it will show him that it is a complicated business needing care and accuracy. In Chapter VI I shall deal more fully with what is, I think, a much easier method, though it has little vogue anywhere, namely, ribband carvel, which combines the features of both the common builds. In any case, we have the basic boat, which is much the same eve-rywhere; let us see how variations on her affect her structural strength.

A boat intended for a centreboard has naturally an extra wide keel, and the cautious builder will carry the sides of the casing, or some other longitudinal stiff-ening, well fore and aft of the slot. But the keel is, after all, not of the first impor-tance; it is the skin of a vessel which keeps her from hogging, or sagging, which it will only do as long as it retains its proper form and its homogeneity. If there are no thwarts to fix the gunwale in its correct curve and position it is fixed more effectively, because at its own level, by deck-beams; or, not always so effectively, by side decks which should serve as webs of girders of which their coamings and the gunwales form the flanges. The efficiency of the side decks depends on their solidarity with those flanges; match-boarding covered with canvas merely to keep the water out does not give enough stiffening to the gunwales.

The homogeneity of a clench-built skin, with overlapping planks nailed together at every three inches, is almost perfect. Not so the carvel skin, for there is nothing except tight caulking to prevent the edges of the planks from sliding on each other, and it is impracticable to caulk the thin planking of a small boat. The planking may be done closely enough to make the boat quite rigid when she is new, but weather conditions—a drying March wind or a hot summer sun after a long spell of wet—in time shrink the plank and open the seams, and her rigidity depends entirely on the widely spaced fastenings of plank to frames. The bottom planking, of course, soon swells once the boat is launched, and the seams close up, but the topsides remain weak and leaky. Nothing except teak will keep really tight there; but it is an immense protection to any sort of wood to paint it white, inside and out. The sun does not shrink a white plank as it does one painted dark or varnished.

After teak, the best plank for a boat is elm—that is, narrow-leaved or wych-elm, for English elm is not durable. It is somewhat heavier than spruce, but makes so much stronger a job that weight can be saved elsewhere. You cannot crush the wood by roving the fastenings too hard, and they can never work loose under a heavy strain. The age of that centenarian boat I mentioned, which is planked with elm, is only shown by the nails and roves, which are of a pattern not used in the last hundred years, and are all present and correct. In her case, tradition says that the timber was seasoned in mud; it is as hard as iron now, but must have been soft and flexible when put on. Generally, elm is used fresh-cut, not seasoned at all; it is then very easy to work, will bend without breaking and twist without splitting, and holds a nail well. The hardness it acquires makes it suitable for clench-built boats which are often beached, for the lands of a soft-wood plank, that is the outer overlapping edges, soon get frayed and broken. Larch is the next best material; it makes a strong, tough plank, and has the useful property of not rotting in fresh water, but it is rather heavy, and the grain is apt to be coarse and irregular, which makes it hard to work.

The boat's bottom should be protected by rubbers or bilge-keels amidships, so placed that when she is resting on one and on the main keel the average-sized stone will not touch her bottom; their depth will depend on the size of stone likely to be encountered. Holly, beech, or oak are the best materials. They are often made too narrow, and then are easily torn off; it is very annoying when the fore end of one gets loose and picks up a rope or other obstruction. If they are to be an inch deep I should make them at least two inches wide, to get a good seating on the plank; then a sideways blow cannot start the fastenings. They should be of half-round section, so that the blow glances off.

The main keel is usually of oak, beech, or elm, but, as it should be protected by an iron band, it is not subject to wear. If the band drops off and the keel gets worn down it doesn't do the boat much harm, but it may leave nails and screws sticking out, and when you try to pull her across a beach on skids they catch and you can't move her. The stem, stern-post, deadwoods, knees, anything that is sawn to shape, are generally oak; the transom elm. Most boat fastenings are copper nails driven right through and roved or clenched, so they cannot draw; but dumps, or common driven nails, must be used for the plank-ends and perhaps the garboards. They will not draw out of oak, and seldom out of elm. The nails of the upper strakes have to go in the end grain of the transom, but elm does not mind that sort of treatment, and they are quite safe there. Nailing is easy if the parts are held tightly together during the process. When putting in a plank you start at the stem, where there is nothing much to hold on to; there is not so much bend at the transom, and if you leave the plank a good bit over-length it makes a handle to hold it in place. Small repair jobs are the difficulty, for it is much harder to bend a short length of plank than a whole long one; it pays to take out a good long piece, or even the whole, of a damaged plank rather than to patch it.

Wych elm, American elm, or ash, are best for steamed timbers. Oak is sometimes used, but its grain is seldom straight enough for it to bend evenly. Ash should only be used for light work; in large scantlings it is liable to rot. Elm, larch, or pitch-pine are good for gunwales.

III

THE ROWING BOAT

THE SCOPE OF THIS BOOK IS LIMITED to such craft as work in the open sea or on large lakes, excluding river skiffs and boats designed for racing in smooth water, and those primarily motor-driven. Ultimately they depend on oars for their propulsion. In most cases it is waste of time to try to sail a boat dead to windward if she is light enough to row and conveniently arranged for that end; and nothing gives such control or power of manoeuvring in awkward places as a pair of oars. But those oars and the position of the thwarts and rowlocks must be as carefully proportioned as the trim of a sailing boat, or rowing will be a penance; and too many men seem to think that any old thing will do for a mere pulling boat, and do not make the best of what she is by attention to her trim.

Owing to the custom of selling boats by the foot they tend to be too short for their form and their other dimensions. Mere lightness is not a virtue except in boats that have to be moved about ashore frequently. Length and steadiness in a lop of sea are the factors that make for speed, and easy lines mean easy pulling; and the longer a boat is the less she is put out of trim by the varying position of the weights in her. For you cannot always put the weights where you want them, as in a sailing boat; extra passengers have to be kept out of the way of the rowers, that is to say, put in her ends; and if her ends are made full to carry them she will be bad to pull when light. Rowing differs from other methods of propulsion in that it is intermittent, and between the strokes there is only the boat's impetus to keep her moving. A light boat with full ends loses way so quickly that half the stroke is wasted in accelerating her. A short boat will go down by the head as the rower's weight moves forward during the stroke. She should then be long enough to obtain plenty of buoyancy in the bows without making them too bluff. I think 12 feet is the smallest useful length for a general-purpose boat.

The proper trim of a boat does not always get the attention it deserves. Even in a flat calm one that is down by the head is heavy to pull and steers badly, and with a cross wind she becomes almost unmanageable. A boat with no way on her drifts sideways to leeward, with no tendency to turn either way; the water exerts

an equal pressure on her bow and her stern. But as she moves ahead the pressure of her lee bow increases and that on her quarter diminishes, and she runs up
into the wind; the amount of this 'ardency' depends on her rate of drift, and that
largely on the proportion of her underwater profile which is at right-angles to the
pressure; the worst offenders are those which have no external keel or deadwood
at all. The fault is cured by increasing the resistance of the stern to drift, by giving
it deeper immersion or a greater area of vertical surface in the form of deadwood.
Practically they come to the same thing, because to increase the deadwood you
have to diminish the after-body of the boat, and any additional weight there puts
it down easily. But if a boat is expected to carry the maximum of weight on the
minimum of length she must not be too sensitive to changes in the position of that
weight, or an extra passenger would depress her stern dangerously; the buoyancy
lost by fining away her run must be compensated for by the reserve buoyancy of
a longer above-water body. This lengthening would bring her transom well above
the water, an advantage so obvious that it seems well worth a pound or two.

Let us consider the seating of a boat 10 to 12 feet long. The stern seat will be
right against the transom; the rowing thwart a little abaft amidships, and the bow
thwart at least 2 feet 7 inches from the midship one, centre to centre. With the
usual spacing—and 2 feet 7 inches is well below the average—the centre of the
bow thwart will be about 27 per cent of the length of a ten-foot boat, and about 35
per cent of a twelve-footer, from her stem. A rower there would need a passenger
of the same weight sitting aft to keep her on an even keel.[1] If, then, there are two
men in the boat one must be a passenger and the other sit up in the bows, where
the narrower beam and increased movement in a seaway make rowing difficult; an
obvious waste of manpower, to say nothing of the fact that a pair of long oars is
infinitely more efficient and less tiring than two pairs of paddles.[2]

I suggest an arrangement by which two men could pull even a ten-foot boat
efficiently. I have never seen it tried, but it could be done experimentally, at small
expense in any boat. You cannot safely shift the thwarts, at any rate the midship
one, for it would weaken the structure, but you can fit extra rowlocks anywhere,

1   Originally, floating with the keel horizontal; also properly used of 'in correct fore-and-aft
    trim'. Often wrongly used to denote 'upright, with no sideways inclination'.
2   In sea usage a man rows with a pair of paddles, not a pair of sculls as on a river.

and ship[1] movable thwarts anywhere to suit them. Bow oar would of course have to be far enough forward to prevent his knees from fouling the fixed midship thwart, but, since this arrangement is only necessary when there are no passengers, stroke oar can go as far aft as is needed to trim the boat. Do not try to economize by making only two extra rowlock fittings, one each side; it is sometimes an immense advantage to be able to get the bow oar to windward.

I have given 2 feet 7 inches as the minimum spacing for thwarts, but in a beamy boat intended usually to be pulled with two oars they may be closer, for the rowers do not sit on the centre line, but well over to each side, out of each other's way. (A good many novices don't understand this, and complain of the weight of the oars. There must be a right proportion between the length of the loom inboard and the length outboard.) A regular 'coxswainless pair' would, however, naturally have her seating arranged so that her normal crew kept her on an even keel, and she would probably be long enough to handle fairly well with one rower on either thwart. A slight variation in trim may at times be useful; for instance, if you have to pull straight against a strong wind a boat that is a trifle down by the head will not be blown off her course.

The proportion of beam to length varies with the size of a boat; she must have enough stability and buoyancy, however small she is, and that is obtained less harmfully by increasing her beam and keeping her ends fine than by making her narrow and wall-sided with bluff ends. Yet I think the majority of boats of about 12 feet length are too wide. Stability is not important in a boat which is not intended for sailing, and buoyancy can be obtained by making her deeper. And for fancy sailing even very narrow craft are possible, if not entirely safe and easy to handle; witness the performance of racing canoes, which depend on the agility of their crews to keep them from capsizing. Worth gives 4 foot 6 inches as the beam of a twelve-footer. I measured the first dozen small boats I saw in the creek I am writing from; they averaged eleven foot seven, so one would expect the proportion of beam to be slightly higher. Reduced to a twelve-footer it worked out at four foot seven and a half. But my own dinghy, which has a beam of 4 feet, is reckoned

---

1   To ship anything is to put it in position for use, except in the case of oars. Different authorities give the phrase 'to ship oars' exactly opposite meanings; it should be avoided, and 'to boat oars' used for laying them inboard.

locally as the best pulling boat of the lot, and I can do some pretty hard sailing in her. The narrower boat, of course, has easier lines, and that, as well as making her faster, makes her easier to build.

It is presumably to make the building easier that so many boats have weak bows. There is no other reason why they should not have bows like any other modern craft, as fine as you like at the waterline—though this can be overdone—but wide enough at the gunwale to keep them from diving into a head sea. A hundred years ago this was the practice in craft of every size, down to the smallest; big steamers have now gone back to it, but the undecked boat, to which a dive is immediately fatal, sticks to a wedge-shaped bow with little reserve buoyancy. I suggest that a good way to get the line for the gunwale is to make the breast-hook a right-angle, fix a flexible batten to it, and let that take its own curve from there to the midship mould. The result may look queer, but it feels safe. Similarly, in a rowing boat, though not in a sailing boat, there is no limit to the width the stern may be above the water, as long as the run, or the after-body below water, is kept fine. But one seldom hears of a boat being swamped by the stern. No boat, unless much overloaded, is likely to ship water amidships; the ends, and especially the bows, should be very considerably higher than that, showing in profile what is called a 'bold sheer', but one too often sees boats with no sheer at all.

But another consideration affects the height amidships; it must be enough to allow the rower to get his oar clear of the water in a choppy sea. In a boat with little freeboard there must be a corresponding increase of the height of the rowlock above the thwart. The height of the thwart above the bottom boards is immaterial, except as it affects the strength of the boat, and that can always be secured by good knees with plenty of fastenings between the thwart and the gunwale. If the rowlock is 15 inches above the water it should be 9 inches above the thwart.

The distance of the rowlock from the after edge of the thwart seems to vary widely. I have measured a number between 9 and 12 inches, but Worth gives 13 and 14; I think 12 is a good figure. Rowlocks may be metal crutches, double thole-pins, or single tholes with the oar held to them by a loop of rope. In some districts single tholes passing through a hole in a wood clamp fixed to the oar are used, but these may be dismissed; feathering is impossible, and you can't shorten your oar to avoid rocks or other obstructions. As far as actual rowing is concerned they all work equally well, except that as the space between the fixed tholes must be greater than the width of a pivoted crutch the oar has a good deal of play and wears quicker. With square rowlocks the looms of the oars might be slightly squared, to take some of the strain of keeping the blades upright off the wrists and fingers, but as far as I know square oars are never used at sea, except those so completely square that they cannot be feathered, though it is the common river practice. Double tholes have the slight disadvantage that if you get the blade of the oar caught anyhow when the boat is travelling fast, and are too slow in lifting it out of the rowlock, you will break a thole-pin or split the gunwale; the after-pin ought to be weak enough to ensure that it is the only thing to break. It is in harbour and beach work that differences between the various patterns of rowlocks appear.

You must not lose a paddle, for instance, when you lean out to pick up a buoy—a thing more difficult than it looks, when the buoy is a heavy one and the wind and tide are strong—or when you come alongside a moored vessel in bad conditions; and when launching off a beach a split second's delay in getting the oars out may mean that the boat is driven back ashore. It is easier to place them between thole-pins than in a pivoted crutch, which is likely to be turned the wrong way. Another argument for tholes is that if they are broken, lost, or stolen, they are easily replaced, which is not so true of crutches; in some ports that is quite a consideration. Some day one will have to get home with a single pin in the crutch socket with a loop of rope to hold the oar. And the single-hander who has found out how well this serves him will adopt it for beach, mooring, or fishing work, though it brings the paddle a couple of inches nearer the thwart than it should be. For if it is placed on the fore side of the thole-pin, so that when rowing ahead you pull against the loop, when you let go the handle the oar will trail overboard safely, flat against the boat's side. The same end can be attained with crutches pivoted at the after side, so that they swivel outboard, but they are not commonly obtainable. If used, the sockets for them must be 2 inches further aft than normal.

The ash oars and paddles sold with small boats are usually of very bad proportions. Their blades are far too wide and heavy, and their looms too thin and light; they are so badly balanced that to make their use possible they are absurdly short. I have a pair of paddles made nearly ten years ago for a boat of 4 feet beam, and I do not see how I could improve on them. They are 8 foot 6 inches long, and the blades are only 4 inches wide, and lightened enough to balance perfectly, though they are ash. I should have preferred fir; it would not have been much less durable, for I could have left them substantially thicker all through without increasing the weight. A single oar should not be less than 11 feet long; a boat intended to be rowed by two men pair-oar will probably be long enough to make the boating of them possible.

Oars should be leathered in the way of the rowlocks, to save wear, and don't make the leathering too short. The rowlock will come in a different place according to which thwart one is rowing from. For that reason, probably, sea oars are never fitted with buttons, leather stops to prevent them from slipping outboard, because they fix the effective length. But for one's private pair of paddles, always to be used in the same place, it would be worth while fitting buttons. These, for a round loom, would be collars made up of two thicknesses of sole-leather nailed on. Do not fix them till you are sure you have got the paddles the right length. Generally, I think the handles should overlap about 4 inches when they are held horizontally and in line, but if that makes the paddles too heavy outboard the overlap may be increased to 8 inches. One often sees people rowing with their oars or paddles too short inboard, which is tiring and inefficient.

Many fishermen and others like to scull their boats with one oar over the stern, even when there is no need to do so. It seems to me a slow and laborious job; but all boats should have a sculling notch in the transom, or a socket for a rowlock, in case one of a pair of oars is lost and there is no spare aboard. The Oriental mechanical sculling device, or yuloh, is quite another matter; it is really efficient, in its place, but the oar used is an enormous and cumbrous affair, and out of place in a boat which can be pulled just as well with a pair of paddles.

IV

THE SAILING BOAT

T HE SAILING BOAT REFERRED TO IN THIS BOOK, which excludes all racing craft, is not a miniature yacht. Their functions are different; the boatman is dependent on the shore, and has to make his port in good time, the yachtsman can keep the sea as long as he likes. But a sailing boat, as I define the term, is not merely a small yacht stripped for action; the significant difference is in the method of handling them. The yacht is almost uncapsizable, and, if luffed head to wind, heavy enough to carry her headway for some little time after the sails have ceased to draw. The boat stops immediately the propelling force fails. In a yacht the main sheet is belayed, keeping the sail at a constant angle with her keel, and to spill the wind out of the sail in a squall she is luffed, or turned towards the wind's eye with the helm. In a boat the main sheet must be held in the hand, and with it she is played through a squall as a fish is played with rod and line, while she is kept sailing smartly all the time. It is fatal to luff, for if she loses headway she will not recover it till she has fallen off broadside to the wind, and if she is caught in that position with no way on she is easily capsized. Then, if the boat's sails have to be taken in, they must come in at once, while in a yacht there is never great hurry about reducing canvas. These considerations limit the size of a boat's mainsail and enjoin simplicity and certainty in working on her gear. As a set-off it should be remembered that the crew can get about their work with far more ease and safety in an open boat than on a small yacht's deck.

Safety first must be the rule in a small vessel, and the safety of a boat often depends on her ability to run for shelter from increasing wind and sea at a good speed. Since any mistake in the steering may be fatal, the boat should ease this task as far as possible by being steady and light on her helm; that is, by being of suitable design and in correct trim. When she is floating upright her trim can be adjusted by shifting crew or ballast, but when sailing she is heeled over, and the immersed part of her hull has quite a different figure; its centre must coincide with her original centre of buoyancy if her trim is to be preserved. That is not to say that her two ends must be identical, but they must not be markedly different; the narrow bows and wide quarters of many old boats make their hulls badly unbalanced. When heeled their bows sink, and at the same time fall slightly to leeward, and their sterns rise, and move a little to windward. Then either of two things may happen: the increased immersion forward may make the boat fly up into the wind, or, if she has a large fin keel, she may follow her nose and run further off the wind. Between them her steering will be most erratic. We cannot restore her balance by widening her bows above water indefinitely, as in a pulling or a power boat, or the lee one may scoop into a sea and swamp her, so we must narrow her quarters. Then, and then only, will she keep a steady course in all conditions.

A boat under sail is subject to other powerful forces. The increased pressure of the water on her lee bow not only pushes that to windward but lifts it, and at the high speed which can be attained by an unballasted craft she climbs out of the water and planes, her stern sinking to an extent dependent on the height of the centre of effort of the sails. I once had a twentyfour-foot whale-boat which, when running at over ten knots—she was capable of twelve—showed only a few inches of freeboard aft, which brought a following sea alarmingly near; but the fact that her stern would sink so far indicated a fine run and narrow quarters, and a consequent absence of wave-making, the chief cause of pooping and of bad steering which leads to broaching to or an unintended gybe. On the other hand, in a short boat with a tall mast well forward in her the depressing effect of the sail-pressure will exceed the lifting effect of the water-pressure; she will go down by the head and become unmanageable, and indeed dangerous with a strong wind abaft the beam.

Boats meant for smooth-water sailing tend to have a lofty rig, for windward efficiency, and great beam, to counteract the leverage of the long mast. But compared with a longer and narrower boat of the same weight and capacity the beamy boat is a poor performer with a free wind, and may be actually dangerous in a rough sea. Her stability is great at small angles of heel, but it soon vanishes. A shallow, flat-floored vessel always floats normal to the surface of the water, at whatever angle that may be; as a steep beam sea passes under her she takes a great list to leeward. As she tops the rise a big expanse of her bilge and bottom is exposed to the wind, and a very small breaking crest on the wave finishes the job of rolling her right over. This has occurred to vessels of some size but of shallow form, which have broached to when running under bare poles. Length as well as beam contributes to stability, but to a lesser extent, and in a degree which varies with the boat's size; a small boat must be proportionately wider than a large one. A twelve-foot boat would hardly have less than 4 feet 3 inches beam—the four-foot beam I advocated in the preceding chapter was for a rowing boat—while my twentyfour-foot whaler had only 6 feet, and she carried more than 200 square feet of sail on long open sea passages, some of them dead plugs to windward. It is a pity that small boats, of every type, are so much the fashion; they are not cheap, for a costly and complicated rig is required to show off their virtues in the one kind of sailing in which they excel. In a seaway, longer craft, more simply rigged, might hold their own even to windward because of their greater speed, and with the wind free there is no comparison. I do not deny that a racing dinghy will plane, and may therefore attain any speed, but it can seldom be safe to allow her to do so. The canoe for which Uffa Fox claims sixteen knots was 17 feet long and 3 feet 6 inches wide. My whaler felt perfectly safe at twelve, with the wind on the quarter, provided there was room to run her off dead before the worst seas.

A long boat, having easier lines, does not want as much sail to drive her as a shorter one of the same weight; and since her sail can be spread out fore and aft instead of towering upwards, her lack of beam is no disadvantage. Her length allows fine lines aft, and the stern is generally allowed to be the most important part of any craft, though, because it is the custom to sell boats by length, it is too often docked most objectionably for the sake of economy. I have a preference for a sharp or whale-boat stern, not due only to sentiment—my whaler was my first and most enduring love—but because it is a safer buy than a transom stern. There are many degrees of suitability in a square stern, and that of the racing dinghy, nearly as wide and flat-bottomed as a speed-boat's, is not suitable for our sea-boat. Her stern should be narrow and triangular in section, so that when she is heeled she puts no more of it into the water than when she is upright. The construction of a sharp stern practically requires such sections, and if they are distorted the result is so conspicuously ugly that the boat is rejected without hesitation. There is no reason why the same sections should not be finished with a narrow triangular transom, which is lighter and cheaper than a sharp stern and has the great advantage of giving the sheets a better lead, but in spite of all logic it isn't done.

A transom should be well above the water when the boat is on an even keel, but if she trims much by the stern when planing it will, of course, be more or less immersed. A slight immersion does not matter, because at high speeds the water leaves the stern cleanly and without eddies and hardly touches the flat transom. But if the immersion is considerable the water pours in behind the transom and a great mass of it is dragged along behind the boat. All this perhaps seems rather theoretical, because common boats very seldom attain planing speeds, but their transoms ought to be small and high enough to keep them out of the water in all normal conditions. It is because this rule is so often neglected that I say the whale-boat is the safer buy.

A word of warning about sailing boats built for rowing only. This is by no means an unprofitable amusement. Neither my twentyfour-footer nor my twelve-footer ever had sails before I bought them, but both proved quite conspicuously successful. But they were not constructed to stand the strains of the masts—in the case of the larger boat pulling against nearly half a ton of crew and ballast—when driven hard, and sooner or later they developed weaknesses. The case of the larger one is the commoner. She was rigged with two lug sails, the mainmast stepped through the second thwart and stayed with wire shrouds. The luff of the jib served as forestay, but the mast thwart showed no tendency to shift fore and aft, for it was connected by a centre plank to the bow thwart. Now that boat's bottom had been stiffened, to resist the strains of grounding, those most likely to occur in the coastguard service, for which she was built, by half-frames or floors between all the common frames, extending as far as the turn of the bilge. When she was sailed hard the shroud pulled her weather side inwards, while the mast thwart pushed her lee side out; the stiffened floor could not bend, so she bent at the turn of the bilge, and in the course of time broke most of the frames along that line. A boat with a hard bilge would be particularly liable to this straining, so some extra strong frames extending from keel to gunwale should be fitted in the way of the mast.

I sailed a twenty-footer during the last war with the whaler's mainsail, which I admit was a bit big for her, on a mast stepped through a thwart; it had no permanent shrouds, the halyards being expected to serve the purpose. That thwart came adrift altogether, being fastened in the usual inadequate way, that is to say, it merely rested on the risings or stringers and was only held in place by single fastenings through the knees and the gunwales seven inches above it. In theory it was kept from shifting fore and aft by having its ends notched to the frames, but they were very thin frames, and rounded at that, so they soon slipped out of the notches. It should have been easy to screw the thwarts down to the risings, and to put a fastening in the knee as low down as possible (Fig. IIc). But builders generally round off the risings as well as the frames. When I build a boat I leave the rising square and thick enough to hold a good fastening; and I make the frame in the way of a thwart, flat and extra wide, and fasten the knee to that as well as to the gunwale. One knee so fitted is stronger than the usual two as usually fitted, and only half as much trouble to make.

As well as the obvious transverse and fore and aft strains a boat under sail is subject to diagonal ones, but it is very exceptional to see these guarded against by fitting horizontal or 'lodging' knees to the thwarts. It is not much trouble to prolong the life of a boat which really suits one and is in other respects well-built, by these simple additions.

A boat of 14 feet or less is I think best rigged with one sail on a mast right up in the eyes of her. There is no thwart there to support it, but we can put in something much better (Fig. IIb). The mast is clamped to a beam fastened across the gunwales. As one of the virtues of an open boat is that you can go unobstructed from end to end in her, this beam is only tolerable right forward, where it impedes neither the working of the ship nor landing on a beach; a mast amidships must be clamped to a common thwart. The exact length of the mast below this beam will of course depend on the shape of the bows, but it is not likely to be less than 18 inches. The length from a thwart to a mast-step under it would be 12 inches or less. That means that the leverage on the forward mast-clamp is only two-thirds of that on a thwart, and the mast will stand up without any stays, which indeed would be useless there, for they would have no spread. The structure is properly triangulated; the mast-beam makes with the gunwales converging to the stem a horizontal triangle, and with the bow frames converging to the keel a vertical one; the mast could hardly move in respect to the stem. But it is now a lever applied to one end only of the boat, not to the middle of her, and it must put a great twisting strain on her. There is no way of counteracting this; she must just be strongly enough built to stand it.

Most people, when they think of a sailing boat, think of a centreboard. But it is not easy to put a centreboard into an old boat without weakening her. One could of course add enough stiffening to make her actually stronger than before, but it is likely to be a clumsy job. It can be made a very much smaller job if one uses a dagger-board or drop keel instead of the pivoted centreboard; the slot in the keel need not be more than a foot or so long. This handy and economical device has only one fault; it does not rise up when it hits a rock, as a centreboard is supposed to do. For that reason I would not make it of metal, which might bend and jam, but of very thin wood, which is certain to break (though in point of fact a boat I built some fifteen years ago has broken only one of them). But the simplest and cheapest way of making a boat sail, because it entails no structural alterations at all to her, is to fit her with a leeboard, as will be described later (p. 76 and Fig. VIID).

When choosing a boat one should ask one's self—though apparently it isn't always done, or there would not be so many misfits—What do I want her for? Is it to get me somewhere, or just to go sailing in? If it's the first, shallow draught is the most desired feature. You haven't got anywhere if you can't reach a landing-place and there isn't a longshoreman within hail. Do not sacrifice your greatest advantage over the owner of the small yacht, which is the most inefficient sort of craft. A good open boat can beat him, except on a turn to windward—and can probably do so then, if he's towing a dinghy nearly as big as his yacht in the open sea. The second essential is lightness. A boat is not a yacht, and it is no good pretending she is by cluttering her up with gear and gadgets. No boat is fit for the sea unless she can be got into port with a pair of oars, but how often one sees perfectly good hulls so loaded and obstructed by vain additions that they cannot be pulled at all! They are given motors, and that damns them, as boats, for all time.

It is not only for the sake of rowing that a boat should be kept light. If she is used on a coast ill-provided with deep-water creeks and harbours she must be beached some time; if in an estuary with a big range of tide she will spend half her time on a mud-bank, and her owner doesn't want to have to wait impotently till she floats. He must be able to haul her up or at least to launch her with the help likely to be available. As a general utility boat she must be strongly built, so her size will be limited by the weight her crew can handle and by the nature of the coast she is used on. My twentyfour-foot whaler was my ideal sailing boat, but we nearly always managed to keep her afloat. If we were left on a sandy beach we were in trouble, because even with all the ballast and spars out of her she was too heavy to move, and of course hauling her up was out of the question. Two of us could handle that twenty-footer I mentioned on a beach, and beaching, if there is any surf, requires a crew of two, even for a much smaller boat, so it looks as if 20 feet was a suitable maximum for that kind of work. She was a very able boat, and put in some hard war-service in a Hebridean winter, though I never had quite the same confidence in her as in the larger whaler.

Both of these were entirely open boats, with no other additions than their centreboards, with the help of which they would work to windward fairly well against the big seas of the Atlantic and even against the chop in the Minch, and they were incredibly fast off the wind. Does any reasonable person want more, unless it be a wholly decked yacht big enough to live aboard? If you are going to camp out under an awning there is more room in a boat 24 feet by 6 than in one 18 by 6 with 6 feet of a rabbit-hutch in the bows of her, which seems to be the popular type. Boat-sailing in a climate where you can't guarantee fine weather must involve some risk of discomfort; do not let vain precautions against it interfere with sailing qualities.

The half-decked boat claims two advantages, one of which is more apparent than real. She throws off any water that may come over the bows—but does anything more than spray come over them? I think before it did it would come over amidships—and that if she has side decks you can safely carry on with the gunwale awash. I question that word 'safely'; side decks are a temptation to heel a shallow boat beyond her limit of stability in a seaway. In fact they reduce potential stability, for the crew does not generally sit right out to windward on them.

The other claim is a good one. The mast is clamped to a deck-beam, not to a thwart; a much stronger job, if the beam is properly fastened; and the same beam stiffens the gunwales against the pull of the shrouds. This is a real sailing boat, with worthwhile rigging, and, so, no mechanical limit to the height of the mast. The owner is tempted to go modern, and ship a towering stick with a tall narrow sail on it. Whether this is a good rig for sea work I shall not discuss here; I am only concerned with the position of the mast. We are free from the small yacht's temptation of putting it right forward to keep it out of the cabin; we can follow the old rule for cutters and put it at two-fifths of the water-line length from the bow, or, since the taller the rig the farther aft the mast should be, even right amidships. But then we are up against a practical difficulty, the disproportion between the sails; the mainsail, safe and easily handled, too small, and the headsail, difficult and dangerous—indeed the most frequent cause of dismasting—too big. Personally I would keep the canvas, of any boat low, so as not to impair her stability, for I want plenty of it, to take advantage of a fair wind, since windward work is apt to be unprofitable; and I would keep the units small, for easy handling. I would rig any boat more than 20 feet long on two masts.

Unless the fittings on the stern absolutely preclude it there ought to be a rowlock on the transom so that if necessary one could steer with an oar. The rudder of a shallow boat, hanging down below the keel, is liable to be broken or lost; or, when she is running before a very steep sea, it may come right out of the water at a critical moment, and let her broach to. On one such occasion I felt that the situation was saved only by a sixteen-foot steering oar. Let it be the longest oar on board. It isn't an easy thing to handle anyway, and unless the boat were very light on her helm would not be much good in a strong beam wind.

Sixteen feet is a good length for a pair of oars for a boat of 6 feet beam, and there should be a 10-foot pair of paddles. But observe that if you have side decks the beam, as far as the rower is concerned, is only the width between the coamings, and wherever you put the rowlocks you do not get a really free use of the oars; another argument, if one were needed, against side decks. Oars may be used only in a calm, but there may be no wind and a great deal of sea, and the tide sweeping you on to a reef; then you want to be able to get your oar into the water and out of it again at the right time, without being hampered by obstructions in the boat.

A boat will handle all right in smooth water without ballast, but it is heartbreaking trying to get her to windward against any sea if she is light. In my twenty-four-foot whaler we carried 5 cwt. in the form of iron 56 lb. weights, rectangular, with fixed handles, very handy for shifting—we trimmed them across when tacking—and useful for mooring, but it was not enough when I was alone in her. Some people object to iron ballast in an open boat. They can use water ballast in petrol tins, which has the advantage that if you are becalmed you can pour the water away. But 20 or 30 take up a lot of space, and you don't want to throw them away at three shillings a time. Good heavy shingle in small sacks makes the best ballast; the empty sacks take up no room, and you can get the shingle almost anywhere.

V

STANDARD RIGS

THE PROBLEM OF SETTING ON A SINGLE MAST a sail which is at once efficient in all conditions of wind and sea, and both handy for manoeuvres and easy to reef or furl, does not admit of a definite solution. It has been approached by half a dozen lines, differing as one quality or another is considered most important. The modern yachtsman plumps for weatherliness in the limited conditions of smooth water and moderate wind. Now smooth water and moderate wind are relative terms; a small boat, if there is any wind at all blowing over open water, will find it rough, and she simply will not sail such close courses as one big enough to disregard the roughness. Supreme weatherliness being, then, an unattainable virtue, the small boat is well advised to concentrate on supreme efficiency with the wind a point free. Again, to a small boat a slight increase of wind appears as a heavy squall, forcing her to shorten sail. I must repeat the difference between her case and that of a yacht, for it is at the root of all boat-sailing. Any one can reef a big decked vessel single-handed, for there is no hurry about it, but the sail of an open boat must come down instantly, and must not come down all over the helmsman's head. Too often this is a pious hope, and the man who sails alone is taking serious risks; which is absurd, for the function of sails is to enable him to proceed when he cannot get a crew to help him with the oars. Let him make his rig safe, or scrap his sails and buy a motor. From that point of view ease of working is the most important quality of a boat's rig, and that calls for sails of moderate size and gear of extreme simplicity.

I shall be told that there is only one possible rig for a boat, and that the Bermuda mainsail is of moderate size and its gear extremely simple. But it is a significant fact that working boats, which cannot pick and choose their weather, unanimously reject it—the common rig all up the Atlantic coast of America is the true Bermudan, quite different from the yachtsman's version of it. In many cases the latter is unsuitable for a small boat, for instance, when the mast has to be unstepped frequently; so let us look at some alternatives to it. Excluding the lateen, which is peculiarly suited to conditions in the Western Mediterranean, the choice between them seems largely a matter of taste and tradition, though, some are more suited to a larger boat and some to a smaller. I cannot say of any that it is absolutely the best, for that depends on its fitness for the work required of it. The finest drawing sail of the lot, the dipping lug, the British version of the lateen, is ruled out by its unhandiness in making tacks; even for fishing boats, where it was once almost universal, it is now obsolescent. There are some half-dozen living types suitable for boats between 12 and 20 feet long—above that I ask for two masts— and in Figs. III and IV I have drawn four of them. My sail areas do not exceed a total of 150 square feet, and 120 in the mainsail; a bit on the cautious side for an eighteen-footer, but I suppose her to be a light, open boat. For a stiffer boat they could be increased without any alteration of the gear by lengthening the spars; I have limited the longest to the length of the boat, which is often a convenience, though not a necessity; and where possible I have avoided a boom, which I think a dangerous nuisance. 120 square feet is about as big a mainsail as I should care to handle in a small boat, and its gear can be extremely simple, as that of a larger sail cannot; but of course the possible size depends a good deal on the stability of the boat and one's facilities for getting at the work. In Chapter XI I suggest a mainsail of 150 feet, but that is for a ketch.

The standing lug (Fig. IIIA), now our national rig, developed from the old dipping lug. To avoid lowering the yard and passing the tack[1] round the mast in stays, the sail was tacked to the foot of the mast instead of to the stem-head, and it became a true fore-and-after, though it does not set quite as well on one tack[2] as on the other. In large craft this is accepted; the mast-head sheave is set athwartships, and the yard always hoisted on the same side of the mast. But if the sheave is set fore and aft it is easy to pull the heel of a small yard round abaft the mast, so that when close-hauled it is always to leeward. Then the sail does not touch the mast, except just at the tack, and so is free from wind eddies; it preserves some of the virtue of the dipping lug, which has the whole of its luff well away from the mast. It is well worth while to shift a standing lug thus, at any rate for a long board;[3] it can often be done without starting anything—make the tack fast right at the foot

---

1   For nomenclature, see Fig. IIIA.

2   'On one tack': having the wind on one particular side, especially when beating to windward.

3   'Board': distance sailed on one tack.

of the mast and it comes easier—though it may be necessary to ease up the tack a little to get the heel of the yard round. On the other hand with the wind abaft the beam the yard should lie to windward of the mast, to spread the sail better and to avoid fouling the rigging.

The yard of a lugsail may be peaked by sweating up the halyards while the tack is held down by a fixed strop or hook, but its leverage is all against the man hoisting; to set the stout sail of 120 square feet he would want a whip on the tye halyard; that is, a single block giving a two-to-one purchase on the single rope that goes over the masthead. An easier way is to hoist the yard to the right height with the tack slack, which could be done with the tye alone, and then peak it by bowsing down the tack. A tackle may not be wanted for this, but if it is it will be a short one, whereas the whip has to be the whole length of the mast. The economy of rope is trivial; what matters is that if the whip is used you have twice as much rope down in the boat when the sail is set, and so twice as much chance of its getting foul and causing an accident. The simplicity of its gear is one of the great virtues of the lug rig; let us by all means keep it simple. Its fault is the difficulty of using a decent-sized jib;[1] for the heel of the yard, projecting forward of the mast, may foul the jib, or even the stay it is set on, unless the mast is a good deal taller than is needed to set the lug, or the bowsprit is inconveniently long. To make matters worse, the mast is generally stepped further forward in a lugger than in other rigs, for her sail is a lifting one. If there is a good rake to the mast it may be right in the eyes of her; and that settles the question of the jib by cutting it out altogether, as I should certainly do in any boat less than fifteen feet long.

The standing lug is a very safe sail for an open boat, because with its simple gear the heavy yard cannot fail to come down when the halyard is let go, whichever side of the mast it is on. But the weight of the yard makes it undesirable that it should fall in the wrong place. I commend to single-handers the semi-automatic balance reef which I have tried. A balance reef is tied up along a diagonal line slanting downwards from the nock of the sail, where it is bent to the heel of the yard, generally to the close-reef cringle on the leach. The yard is hung up and down the mast, and the diagonal line becomes the foot of a triangular sail. It

---

1   I have throughout called a single headsail a jib, though this is not strictly correct; for the word 'foresail' without qualification is ambiguous.

is made the same length as the foot of the unreefed sail, so that the reef cringle comes in the same place as the clew did, but of course the sheet has to be shifted to the cringle to set the sail properly, as the clew now comes 2 or 3 feet too far aft. However, in an emergency one could carry on without shifting the sheet or tying the points, because nearly half the sail would be down in the boat, where it could hardly capsize her. To make the device work almost automatically two extra items of gear are wanted: an upper halyard spliced to a thimble which slides on a wire jackstay stretched from the slings, the point where the main halyard is bent on, to the peak of the yard. It is belayed at such a length that when the peak is hanging from it and the main halyard has been let go the heel of the yard is at the level of the tack of the whole sail. At this point there must be a block through which a heel-rope on the yard is rove to hold it in to the mast. Merely letting go the main halyard and hauling in the heel-rope should make it safe for the helmsman to leave the ship to look after herself while he reefs her properly. But a feature of this rig is the ease with which a small lug with a shorter yard can be substituted for the big one instead of reefing; not a great extravagance, for the big sail and its yard would be of lighter stuff and therefore more efficient in light winds, and it would need no reef cringles and points, linings, and so on.

Fig. IIIA shows roughly the Loch Fyne skiff, general in the West of Scotland; but the skiff, having a sharp stern, has a shorter foot to her sail. The one I have drawn could not be sheeted properly except to the lee quarter of a transom stern. In a small boat there is no need to work two main sheets, as in the skiff. A single sheet is bent to the clew of the sail and leads through a block travelling on a horse, an iron bar over the transom, above the tiller, to the helmsman's hand (Fig. IIA). It is no more trouble than the sheet of a boom sail, which is bent to a traveller on the horse and leads through a block on the boom to his hand, except that it prevents passengers from sitting in the stern. If the leach of the sail is fairly upright the clew will not menace people's heads; anyway there is no need for a block on it. Some purchase may be wanted to sheet a sail of 120 square feet, but if there is a big brass thimble in the clew cringle that will do for a block. No one who has sailed without a boom wants to be dependent on one again, but a temporary one is useful in a light following wind; the boathook can serve for it. If the standing part of the sheet is made fast to the lead block, unbend it—you will not want the

purchase in light weather—and hitch it to the clew so as to form a bight or loop
into which you can hook the boathook; the stave should be pointed, to stick into
a rope strop doubled round the mast, like the snotter of a sprit. This temporary
boom can be unshipped in a moment, leaving the sail to be trimmed by the single
sheet in the usual way.

The spritsail is one of the commonest and most widely distributed rigs for
small boats. In its simplest form it requires the minimum of gear, which com-
mends it for working craft. The sail is permanently bent to a short mast; to set
it you merely stick the pointed top end of the sprit into a rope cringle at its peak,
and the pointed butt end into a rope strop on the mast, called a snotter. To reduce
its area in a squall you merely remove the sprit, the peak of the sail blows away
to leeward, and you have a triangular piece left, with no need to shift the sheet
to trim it properly. The sprit is a long spar, but it can be a light one. It is the ideal
rig for a job like whaling, where all the sailing gear has to be cleared away and the
mast lowered in a moment. But it is not the ideal rig for the single-hander, who
has to go forward and unship the sprit out of the snotter by hand; that is not hard
if it is to windward of the sail, but not so easy if to leeward, with the belly of the
sail pressing on it; moreover, when the heel is out of the snotter it has a tendency
to drive down and may go through the boat's bottom. In larger vessels the sprit
is left standing and the sail is brailed in to the mast; in the notoriously squally
Ægean a standing wire lift supports the peak of the sprit, and the head of the sail
is hanked to the lift and hauled out along it. The rig drawn in Fig. IIIb, which I am
considering here, is for a boat of medium size; the sail reefs on the foot, it and the
sprit being lowered down the mast.

It misses much of the simplicity of the smaller size. Not only is a main halyard
wanted but the heel of the sprit has to be hung from the masthead, requiring another sheave up there, for a movable snotter could not be trusted not to slip down,
and, besides, the sprit is a bit heavy for manhandling. It must be compared not
with the simpler lug but with the equally complicated gaff rig.

The spritsail is said to be more close-winded than the gaff sail, which is probably true if the angle of the spar extending the peak of each is the deciding factor;
for the spritsail is equivalent to a very high-peaked gaff sail with a topsail over it.
Further, the spritsail may be of any shape, since its set depends not on the angle

of its head but on that of the sprit, and the mast may be low, and lighter than for other rigs, since the thrust of the sprit comes so low down on it. It must not come too low, however, if the sail reefs on the foot, or a shorter sprit would have to be substituted to allow it to come down low enough for the close reef. Sometimes for a small sail with only one reef in it the snotter is a fixture on the mast and a shorter sprit is shipped for the reef. As the head-rope of the sail is all the support a lowering sprit has, it and the mast-hoop to which it is attached must be amply strong.

My drawing shows a mast a foot shorter than the lugger's, but setting a bigger jib. The sprit is some 4 feet longer than the lug yard, but need weigh no more; the total weight of spars in the sprit rig would probably be less, and is certainly kept lower, as is the peak of the sail also; though it is a more pressing sail than the lug it would be better suited to a boat with poor stability.

The gaff rig is not popular for boats. Men like a boomless sail to have a long head and a short foot, which is less pressing than a gaff mainsail of the usual shape, and less obstructive to the handling of the boat; but such a sail is definitely not so close-winded as a lug or a sprit, the masthead is so much spar wasted, and the gear, as commonly rigged, complicated. It is curious that none of the examples which survive in England—bawleys, Itchen ferry boats (probably extinct), Plymouth hookers, and their like, take advantage of vangs to make the sails set on a wind, and that they all use two halyards where one will do. The 30-foot gaff of the Norfolk wherry, which has to be cleared away and got up again when the mast is lowered for shooting bridges, is hoisted with a single halyard; so is the smaller gaff of the whale-boat used in the Azores. In the Norfolk rig, as simplified for a 10-foot gaff (Fig. IVA), the halyard leads through a masthead block down to a single block on the gaff jaws, up to another masthead block, and is made fast to the peak; since there is a two-to-one purchase on the throat and none on the peak, the luff of the sail is stretched before the peak is set up.

The tye halyard of the Azorean whale-boat is made fast to a span, with one leg on the jaws of the gaff and the other a little in from the peak, at such a point that when the span is hauled tight up to the masthead sheave the gaff is held at the correct angle. Of course unless it is right up, the gaff will not peak properly. I did not notice if the sail was made to reef; if so, the span would have to be held in to the mast, preferably by a running parrel, which is simply a slip noose embracing the halyard and mast, hauled taut after the sail is hoisted. For a small sail without a boom this would be handier than the wherry halyard with its three sheaves aloft.

In favour of separate throat and peak halyards is the fact that you can drop the peak to ease the boat in a squall, or for a gybe in a strong wind; a gaff goes over in a gybe with much more of a bang than a high-peaked lug yard does. There is also the matter of taking in the sail. A gaff has a great tendency to get over the side, and unless it has a vang on the end of it there is nothing very good to haul it in with. I get over the difficulty in this way; I let go the throat halyards altogether, so that the gaff hangs by the peak straight up and down the mast, pull the sail forward out of the way of the helmsman, and get a gasket round it and the gaff—the gasket is a fathom of line made fast by its middle to the jaws so that it is always there ready for use, and I have only to knot the two ends together round the sail—and I can lower the gaff at my leisure. Of course the jaws must be so designed that they are not broken or unshipped by this action. This method would probably work as well with the Norfolk rig, if there were a down-haul made fast to the jaws.

It is barbarous to try to trim a quadrilateral sail by a sheet at one corner only. Unless it is hauled as flat as a board—and however well that may suit racing yachts in smooth water a sea-boat won't sail like that—the head and the foot make quite different angles with the wind, and only a narrow strip in the middle has the right aspect. A vertical section through the sail shows a very considerable inclination; with the heel of the vessel added this may amount to as much as forty-five degrees, that is to say that half the pressure of the wind is merely forcing the boat down into the water. That is what is called a pressing sail. If it could be trimmed by the head as well as by the foot all of it would be equally effective for propulsion; it might even be, as in the case of a squaresail or a lateen, where practically all the trimming is done with the yard, a lifting sail. That is no figure of speech. I have seen a small craft under a squaresail literally lifted by a fresh gale over a sea which my mate, an experienced schooner man, said would have overwhelmed a fore-and-after of many times her size. We could get some of this lifting effect with a sail trimmed by vangs on the gaff. It is a pleasure to look at and a joy to handle. One can ease off the sheet till the foot of the sail takes a handsome flow, for there is no great strain on it; but just for that reason I fear vangs are forbidden to the boat sailor, because letting go the sheet does not spill the wind out of the upper part of the sail unless the vang is let go too, and my definition of a boat, as distinct from a yacht, was that she should be sailed with the sheet. However, a vang is so useful in other ways, to help in getting in the sail, and to steady the ship and save her gear when running before the wind, that I must make this plea for it: if the gaff is held in taut the main-sheet can be belayed so easy that letting go the vang would spill a squall effectually out of the dangerous part of the sail.

I shall be asked just how much difference there is between the lead of a vang from the peak to the weather quarter and that of the leach of the sail and the sheet to the lee quarter. Personally I found vangs 40 feet long on a stern 5 feet wide extremely effective. A transom 3 feet wide with the peak 18 feet above it is a more likely proportion; the difference in angle from the two ends of the transom is then ten degrees. But that is not the point. If you could pull the leach of the sail into a dead straight line, which would take a prodigious drag, you would spoil the sail for anything except an ultra-close-hauled course in absolutely smooth water, whereas with a single rope as a vang I could pull the 20-foot gaff of my yacht right amidships, if necessary, and trim the sheet as required to suit the strength and direction of the wind.

Without a vang the head of the sail must sag to leeward more or less; how do we ensure that it sags less? The pundits say that the angle of the peak influences it. This I do not believe. I think what makes the difference is the height of the peak halyards on the mast; and that is the snare of the bald-headed gaff rig—to save a couple of feet of masthead the set of the sail is ruined. One yacht designer, Mr. Laurent Giles, seems to agree with me; he gives his craft handsome tall masts, and to make assurance doubly sure fine big gaff topsails over rather small mainsails. Everyone who has seen it must have noticed how well a reefed mainsail sets with a topsail over it; that is equivalent to raising the peak halyards. It is the sailplan everyone would like, but the three extra ropes needed to set a topsail put it out of court for us, and exclude it from this chapter on standard rigs. In Chapter XII shall suggest a way in which a topsail might be set with only one extra rope, though I have neither seen nor heard of its actual trial. There I shall also show how the same shape can be attained with the one-piece sail which I call a Guntersprit; this sail appears to have been adopted by the Bembridge Sailing Club in 1889, but I have never seen any example except my own.

It is strange that the simplest of all sails, a triangle spread between a mast and a boom, seems to have practically no history in Europe or Asia. Possibly the discoverers of Brazil found the Indians there sailing their centreboard rafts with it, as they do to-day; at any rate it is characteristic not only of Bermuda but of all the Americas. However, it has come here in racing boats, and as yachtsmen always copy the last thing in racers, whether it suits their needs or no, it flourishes in 'pleasure boats', though real working boats, the few that stick to sail, will have none of it.

The same sail may be set in three different ways: as a Bermudan, as a sliding gunter, and as a gunter lug. Whatever may be the merits of the modern so-called Bermudan for racing, its complicated rigging and unreliable track and slides put it out of court for a sea-boat. That it goes to windward so marvellously is largely due to the care and cost lavished on cutting down its gear below the limit of convenience and sometimes below that of safety, and to the almost unlimited height of mast employed. This may be all right for smooth water, but in the open sea a small boat can never be sailed very close to the wind, and is seldom driven hard on any windward course; and a low wide-headed rig is better on a free reach. But since people insist on a triangular mainsail let us see if it can be rigged in a more seamanlike way. The true Bermuda sail, hooped to a mast which is stayed only at its extremity—the typical rig of working boats all up the Atlantic coast—is entirely seamanlike, but the long mast with no intermediate stays must be very stout to resist buckling. The Sliding Gunter rig makes two parts of the mast, stayed at two-thirds of the total height.

The Sliding Gunter (Fig. IVB) was rightly popular for Navy boats, for it is safe and easy-working. The topmast or yard must come down when the halyard is let go; it cannot jam if the sail blows round the mast, as slides do on a track, for it blows round too; it cannot blow away like the yard of a gunter lug, for its two hoops hold it firmly up and down the lower mast, so it will look after itself while being reefed; for a quick furl the clew outhaul is let go and the sail is brailed in to the mast, the height of which is at once reduced by one-third. Naturally the topmast must be heavier than the corresponding part of the Bermuda mast, for it has to stand without stays or shrouds, and one-third of its length is doubled on the lower mast. But that is a small price to pay for its safety and convenience.

No one could suggest that the far more popular gunter lug was in any way an improvement on the true sliding gunter. Its existence can only be explained by the supposition that the people who devised it had never heard of a sliding gunter. The lug-sail is our national rig. Its yard became more and more peaked, till it stood right up and down the mast; to keep it there jaws were fitted at its heel, but it is still only supported aloft by the halyard. It looks very nice when it is properly set, but it is a job to set it, and as soon as you start the halyard it all goes adrift. I know there's generally a running parrel on the slings, but once that gets loose it won't pull the yard up to the mast against a breeze of wind. Why not replace that parrel with an iron one that can't get loose? Because, unless you can let go the clew outhaul, which you cannot do with a roller reefing boom, or unless the hoist of the yard is greater than the length of the boom, which is rarely the case, you can't brail the sail in to the mast, but you have to lower the yard in order to stow it. To disconnect the upper hoop or gunter-iron, as it is called, is not always easy when the yard is swinging round the mast, as is its way, and to connect it again is often quite difficult. The gunter-iron is fixed on the yard; the handiest pattern of mast-hoop is hinged so that it opens at one side; this hinged part is used as a handle to pull it into the mast and clamp it there, and locked with a pin (Fig. IXD). But in the Balearic Islands, where this is the commonest rig for small yachts, the upper gunter-iron connects and disconnects automatically (Fig. IVB). There is a separate complete mast-band, the halyard is attached to this and then rove through a horizontal eye or a sheave on the yard-band, and so to the masthead; as you hoist the two bands are drawn together and locked. The actual locking must be done by a short bit of chain spliced to the end of the rope halyard—you can splice a 1½-in. rope to 3/16-in. long-link chain and it will render easily through a ⅝-in. eye—or by an iron fitting such as that illustrated, to save chafing the rope. The heel-iron shown allows the yard to be lowered horizontal with no chance of coming adrift from the mast.

It is easier to make a sail with a short gaff or none and a longish boom, giving a sloping leach, set on a wind, than one with a long gaff and upright leach, but the virtues of the short-headed sail hardly justify in a small boat the amount of gear needed for the regular cutter rig. For a quadrilateral boom sail set with the minimum of gear the balance lug is much favoured. It has a wide distribution,

and is probably the most ancient form of fore-and-aft sail. It has been the only sail
in China from time immemorial, and at some unknown period it evolved from
the ancient Egyptian squaresail, the foot of which was laced to a boom; if the
boom was tacked down by one end instead of by the middle it became exactly the
present-day *naggar* rig of the Nile. It is now the commonest sail in the Adriatic
and Ægean for small coasters. There is no need to fit it, as in China, with battens
running right across it parallel to the boom; they are no doubt a convenience for
reefing the huge Chinese lugs, but in a small boat they are not wanted either for
reefing or to make the sail set flat. The latter object is secured by the bending
of the boom, to which the sail is laced. The boom, like the yard, extends about
a quarter of its length forward of the mast, to which it is not attached; it is only
held down to the deck by a tack tackle. A sail attached thus, not, as a gaffsail, by
one edge, tends to lie in one plane. In most cases it is always set on the same side
of the mast; being a flatter sail it is less spoiled by this than the loose-footed lug.
But in a small boat it would not be impossible to dip it, boom and all, round the
mast for a long tack; it is a less pressing as well as a better driving sail when it is to
leeward.

Here are six standard rigs to choose from—five if the Bermudan and sliding
gunter are counted as one. For the smallest boats the simplest rig is the best, and
that is, I feel sure, the standing lug as I use it in my own dinghy (Fig. VIIE). It pulls
surprisingly well as close to the wind as my boat has any use for—say four-and-a-
half points off, in smooth water. A word about ultra-close-hauled work, and profitable sail-trimming in general. When a main boom is pinned in dead amidships
most of the sail is doing no good at all; only a narrow strip along the luff, where a
well-cut sail has a decided belly, has the right aspect to the wind. The enormously
long luff of the Bermuda sail makes this useful part large in proportion to the in-
ert or harmful part; therefore it will propel a boat far closer to the wind than any
other sail. But hull resistance, windage of spars, or a head sea, may put a practical limit to a windward course at a point at which it is mechanically possible to
make a great deal more of the sail useful. The average boat never gets beyond that
point, so her problem is to make the whole of the sail useful at it. This cannot be
done merely by easing the main sheet a trifle; the head of the sail sags to leeward,
whether it is extended by a gaff or no, and part of it goes out of business before the

foot becomes useful. Ability to keep the whole of the sail in one plane becomes more important than length of luff. Hence the use of vangs. If they are ruled out I think a lug yard hoisted to leeward of the mast sags least. But note that a boomless sail, unless steadied by a vang, makes a boat roll badly in a following wind.

The virtues of simplicity are relative. A certain lavishness of gear which might be allowed in a boat with no other purpose than sailing, would be inconvenient in one used for a camping cruise and dangerous in one used for fishing; also there is the question of lowering the mast and proceeding under oars. To that extent the choice of rig depends on the boat's function.

Another point concerns the care of sails when not in use. Are they left in the boat, carried ashore spars and all, or unbent? A lug yard or a gaff can be stripped in an instant, if bent as I describe (p. 101 and Fig. XIA); a Bermudan runs off its track (use my spring shackle, p. 99 and Fig. IXB); the mast lacings of the gaff and sprit sails are short. Those sails have the best expectation of life. The gunter yard has an iron in the middle which permanently-tied rovings will not slip past, and the balance lug has to be carefully bent to its boom, so those spars would go ashore with the sails if they did not have to be carried far. A small consideration, but it might affect one's choice.

I have dismissed the dipping lug as a working sail, but it has its use when there is no question of making tacks. It is futile to beat to windward in a boat with neither centreboard nor leeboard, but it is needless to labour at the oars when there is a leading wind. Then we want that sail which is most efficient purely as a sail. With it a common boat should make good her course on 20 out of the 32 points of the compass; so if, by pulling a short distance dead to windward you can bring your destination 6 points on your bow you will reach it quicker by doing so and sailing the rest of the way than by rowing all the way. As the boat will probably be deficient in stability the sail is best made low, with a yard as long as will stow inboard; almost, if not actually, a lateen.

VI

RIBBAND CARVEL[1]

IT WOULD BE SUPERFLUOUS FOR ME TO DESCRIBE in detail the building of a common clench boat; that would be merely to repeat such standard works as R. C. Leslie's *The Sea Boat*, and moreover I should advise the complete beginner to try his hand on an easier job, which is the subject of this chapter. I must confess that it is published entirely without authority; I never saw a ribband carvel boat built, nor read a description of one, but as I have produced three of them with some success and relatively little trouble I shall describe how I did it. Purely by chance the last of them was of a design which made the construction particularly easy, so I commend to the amateur a study of her lines as well. She was unlike any other boat, but she satisfied the conditions of her employment, and in addition she was a good general purpose craft, fast and seaworthy.

The boat was required for an estuary with muddy foreshores, a big range of tide, and strong currents and often rough water—common enough conditions, but seldom taken into account by designers. Her bow had to be pushed up on a mud-bank without ploughing into it, her bottom had to toboggan down it without sticking, and her stern had not to blow round like a weathercock when she was pulled across a fresh wind, which last forbade anything in the shape of a pram. As she could not have an external keel her flat bottom had to be as long as possible. With an overall length of 11 feet her straight keel-plank was about 9 feet long. Her beam was 3 feet 9 inches, and her floor amidships quite flat for a width of some 18 inches. She had a sharp cutwater, to get through the prevalent choppy seas, but below it the forefoot was full and rounded. The V-shaped sections of her long fine run were carried out to the raked tuck of a dog-legged stern-post; there was hardly any reverse curve between the garboards and the triangular transom. Because of this the garboards were easy to fit; aft they had only a twist of some forty-five degrees, and forward they were made narrow to work round the forefoot. This, and the fact that the flat floor ran so far forward, made it necessary to cut the next planks with a big curve at the fore end. For economy they might have been made

---

1   See Fig. V for details.

in two pieces, joined with a butt-strap, a short piece of hard wood covering the join, for a scarf where it was constantly touching the ground would not be a sound job. After the flat part of the floor the planking became easy.

Building started with the keel-plank, of oak ¾-in. thick, 3-in. wide amidships tapering to the ends, with a ⅜-in. rabbet cut on the under side to take the edge of the garboards. The stem and stern-posts were set up. The oak stem had a good curve in the grain, and was thick enough to cut the rabbet for the plank-ends and the notches for the ends of the ribbands; its siding was increased to twice that at the lower end, which was long enough to take two stout copper fastenings clenched on heavy roves in the keel, so a knee was not wanted to connect them. The toe of the stern-post was also left well over-size, and was long enough to take two keel fastenings. Do not cut the notches or shape the forefoot and stern-post yet. When all the frame is finished and the boat can be turned upside down you can see how the ends of the planks come easiest on them; you can then shape them with a chisel and continue the rabbet round them. The notches on the stem need not be cut down into the rabbet, for the ends of the ribbands can be cut slanting to fit them; the housing is not for strength, only to keep the water out. It is easier to run the notches on the stern-post out straight, and mitre the ribbands flush with its feather edge; the plank covers the whole of that.

I used only five oak frames, sawn out of stuff with such true grain that the midship ones ran in one piece from the gunwale right across the flat floor and were amply strong with a section about one inch square; they were fastened together side by side over the floor for extra strength, and nailed to the keel. Generally a 'grown frame' is made of three pieces, the floor and two top timbers, overlapping about 9 inches and side-fastened together at the turn of the bilges (Fig. IIE). With the transom I had now the form of a boat, but it had no rigidity. I placed the keel on a 7-in. by 3-in. deal, fixed up on its edge, and held it down to the deal with strong screws. Battens were nailed across the tops of the frames to keep them in shape, and a stronger batten from stem to transom to hold these together and mark the centre line; the centres of the transverse battens were brought to this and fixed there, and the structure was stiff enough to bend the ½-in. oak sheer-strake round it. This was fastened to the frames and at its ends for a full due.

I made sure that the fore-and-aft batten was securely nailed to stem and transom before unscrewing the keel from the deal foundation, for if anything slipped the keel would bend up in the middle. There was no pull on the screws, and the structure would stand fairly rough handling, so I lifted it and turned it upside down for convenience in fitting the ribbands and planks. Actually there were no ribbands in the flat part of the floor, but double planking; I could not get suitable elm, and was using ⅜-inch pine, a single thickness of which might have been pierced if the boat had sat on a stone, but the principle was the same; it was just that the ribbands were 3 or 4 inches wide and of pine instead of 1 inch wide and of oak, as they were from the bilges up. Note that a layer of calico or brown paper well soaked in paint should be put between the two skins to prevent water seeping in and starting rot. But I do not recommend double-skin work, which is a more troublesome job, if single planking in conjunction with ribbands is strong enough. My shipwright reminds me to insert a warning against buying an old double-skin boat. You cannot be sure that the skins are stuck together with paint all over, and if there is a gap rot will start there; moreover, if there is a leak you cannot trace it.

Fastenings in soft wood have to be roved, as also do the heavy ones in the keel, knees, and the like, so a word about roving. See that the roves are big enough to be a driving fit on the nails, but not tighter, or you may bend the nails. If the roves are a trifle slack the roving iron makes them grip by flattening their conical shape, but don't flatten them too much, or they may cone the wrong way, which crushes the wood and gives less bearing on it. The roving iron is simply a short bolt with a hole drilled up in the end of it; the hole ought not to be much bigger than the nail, because it is wanted to push down the apex of the coned rove, not its skirts. For single-handed work it is a great convenience to have a good heavy iron; drive the nail only till its tapered point comes through, hold the rove over that with the iron, and then go on driving, and you won't lose any roves. The end of the nail must be cut off just clear of the rove; a very little spreading makes it hold, and if you cut it too long and have to hammer it a lot you may bend it. Use a light hammer for the job, and hold a heavy one behind the head of the nail, or the smooth flat butt of the roving-iron, if it is heavy enough, or a common flat-iron may be the handiest tool.

Copper nails may be turned and clenched in hard woods, a far quicker job and said to be just as strong. A clenched nail shows a short length turned down flat along the grain of the wood and hammered down flush with it, the point being turned down further still and driven into the wood. The trick is to make this hooked point just the right length; if it is too long it won't go into a hard wood like oak. A copper nail won't go far unless there is a hole ready for it to go into. Drive the nail till about a quarter of an inch of its point shows; turn that over in the right direction, drive the nail right home, and then turn the main part of it down. You may be able to do the turning down with your left hand while you are driving the nail with your right: you want a heavy hammer-head with a good square edge, or preferably the flat-iron; hold this slanting over the place the nail will come through and it will start the bend the right way; now press the edge of your iron down on the point of the nail, and the next stroke of the hammer will make it into a nice loop which a couple more strokes will flatten down.

The professional will tell you that the frames ought to be notched for the ribbands, so that the planks will lie close on the backs of them, but I see no need for this. The frames of common clench-built boats are not notched, and their planks are just as wide and not so well supported; and there is a reason, if a slovenly one, for not notching them in ribband carvel work. I fasten my ribbands, of oak or elm 1-in. wide and ⅜-in. thick, reduced to ¼-in. at the ends, one at a time, beginning from the keel, to stem and stern, but not to the frames, though those which have a decided bend will have to be held in place temporarily by tacks or cramps. Then I fit the bottom edge of my plank to the one below it. The top edge may, or more probably may not, come accurately on the centre line of the ribband; if it doesn't it's easier to shift the ribband up or down a trifle than to take off the plank and plane it to shape. Then I put a nail through plank, ribband, and frame, and clench it, fasten the plank all along top and bottom to the ribbands, and it is finished with. Actually I tacked filling pieces to the backs of the frames, between the ribbands; but that was for economy, not for strength. A lot of paint would have run into the spaces and been wasted, and a lot of sand and dust can never be cleaned out of them till it runs out mixed with the paint and spoils the work.

I said that some of the ribbands will have to be bent. You can't bend them very much without buckling them, as they are some 2 feet clear between the frames, and not tightly fastened to them, anyway; and you mustn't try, or you will have to cut the plank to impossible curves to follow them. The planks will soon straighten out any tendency the ribbands have to curl up at the edges, even before all the fastenings are in, if the parts are tightly cramped together. It is easy to cramp the top edge of a plank to its ribband, because you are holding it less than an inch in from the edge of the work; you can get small screw cramps at Woolworth's that will do it, or use wooden wedge cramps, Pattern A. It is not so easy to hold the bottom edge, which may be 4 inches in, and you have to do that before the plank is fastened anywhere. Large screw cramps are expensive and difficult to work with one hand; the lever cramp, Pattern B, is easier. But I should have at least one large screw cramp, to hold the fore end of the plank; if you put it abaft the stem it can't slip off.

Ribband carvel certainly needs more plank nails than clench work, but not twice as many, for they may be spaced more widely. To avoid making two holes close together in the ribband I put them alternately top and bottom, the lower edge of the plank not being nailed to the frame. The planks have nominally a half-inch lap on the ribbands, but if the nail-holes are made with a slight slant they can be started half an inch from the edge and still come through nearly at the centre of the ribband. This allows more margin of inaccuracy than other methods, and the planks do not have to be shaped so carefully to make a strong and watertight job. As the seams are, or should be, invisible outside, the layout of the planking does not matter, unless you look inside the boat, when the ribbands are rather more conspicuous than the plank edges in clench work. Without shame I let mine go any way they liked, and even used a couple of stealers; but that is a matter of personal taste.

The sheer-strake being already fastened to the frames I had to bring the next strake below, which would naturally be the thickness of the ribbands away from them, flush with it. As the two were of different thicknesses I did it by fastening both to a half-round oak beading or rubbing strake one inch wide outside them. If one wanted the boat to show a smooth side, the two planks would have to be the same thickness, joined by a ribband inside put in between the frames in sections. The sheer-strake was really stiff enough to do without gunwales, but I put them in to hide the tops of the frames; they were an inch square amidships, so that they did not have to be thickened to take the sockets for the rowlocks, but were reduced in thickness towards the ends. The risings were 1-in. by ⅝-in., which was quite enough to carry the thwarts, because one of these came right on the midship frame and the other close alongside the next frame forward of it. The risings extended right to the stem and were fastened to it with a breast-hook by a strong eyebolt with the eye outside the stem. This is my usual practice for a boat which is going to be left on moorings in a rough place. If you make the mooring fast inboard, it and the gunwale get cut; shackle it to the eye-bolt and there is no chafe. In this particular boat the eye-bolt had another function. She might have to be towed, and a flat-bottomed boat tows badly in a breeze—I have seen one blow round at right angles to the course, and be pulled right over—and she had no keel to make the tow-rope fast to, so that it would tip her up on her sharp heel and keep her straight behind the towing vessel. It was at least better to tow from part way down the stem than from the top of it. Note that if you think of adopting this dodge the eye should be as small as possible, tight up against the stem, and set horizontally; then a sideways pull is not so likely to bend the bolt and split the stem. But stems are not generally wide enough to take a decent-sized bolt.

I built this boat very near a saw-mill which had a good stock of small oak crooks, and could cut them roughly to the shapes I wanted, but what were to me economies in the way of weight and material would not be so everywhere. For instance, the stem was wide enough to dispense with deadwood and apron-piece for fastening the plank ends to; its lower end was more than 3 inches wide, to form the rounded forefoot on which several ribbands and planks converged; a narrower stem would have to be padded out with cheeks to fasten them to. Then the lovely curves of those grown frames enabled me to start planking on them straight away, instead of messing about with temporary moulds and bending in steamed frames later, and made the job rigid enough from the beginning to turn it upside down or shift it to whatever position was handiest for working at.

Ordinary carvel work has these advantages over clench build: it is less liable to external damage, it is easier to take out and replace a damaged plank, it wastes less paint and is easier to keep clean, and the planks can be cut out more economically. On the other hand it is liable to leak in hot weather, it wants much closer framing, and the framing must all be finished before the planking is begun.

That means either a very large number of grown frames, which are hard to obtain and laborious to cut to shape, or considerably more temporary work in the way of moulds and ribbands to bend in steamed frames than if they could be left till the planking is completed—you want more moulds, because the unsupported length of the ribband between them is liable to be displaced when you press down the frame against it, and closely-spaced ribbands, or the frame may form bulges between them.

Ribband carvel construction seems more logical. Timber occurs in long narrow strips, better suited for the long easy curves of ribbands than the short sharp ones of transverse frames. From the practical point of view it cannot leak; it is stronger than clench work, in which some of the thickness of the plank is cut away by bevels, because all the fastenings are in the whole thickness; all the skin can be shaped on three moulds and the few frames needed bent in after the planking is complete; and as for cleaning and painting internally, if it is not so good as common carvel it is no worse than clench. Why it is unpopular is, like many other things connected with boats, a mystery.

VII

A CANVAS CANOE[1]

THE CREWS WHO FISH OFF THE IRISH COAST in big canvas-covered curraghs, locally called canoes, say that no wooden boat could land or be launched on the beaches they have to use, nor live in the sea they have to face; and this is no idle claim, for the canoe is very light and supremely seaworthy. An amateur who wanted a small craft which combined those qualities might be interested in a reduced copy of the fishing canoe, for use in waters not too full of snags or sharp stones. A moderately stony beach will not hurt her, for one never has to drag her up it; a man can pick up a ten-foot boat, capsize her on his shoulders, and walk away with her—unless the wind is strong enough to blow him off his legs. This is how it is done. Lay the oars parallel on the beach, two or three feet apart, and, standing between them, bring the boat's bilge over the blades. Put one foot on the near gunwale, and lift the further gunwale by a short rope made fast to it, rolling her up towards you on the oars, which prevent her from rocking fore and aft. Stoop down, and she will fall on your shoulders, stand up, and walk away with her, dragging the oars after you with a lashing, or they may be washed away before you have deposited the boat in a place of safety. I might add that this is the only way one man can capsize any sort of boat on a beach; if he lifts the near gunwale he is left the wrong side of it shouting for help to ease it down on the other side.

To acquire a canoe you have to build her yourself, but fortunately that is not difficult. My method is not exactly that used by the professional, but it has served for three boats. The building is not started from a keel, for there is no keel—what I call for clarity the 'keel-plank' is merely the central one of a score of longitudinal ribbands over which the canvas is stretched, though it is conveniently made wider than the rest—but from a strong horizontal frame at the level of the thwarts, which I shall call the 'foundation'. This is made up of two curved stringers, corresponding to the risings of a common boat, joined forward by a breast-hook and aft by a transom—using this word in the shipwright's sense of the horizontal mem-

---

1   See Fig. VI for details.

ber of the stern frame. The bottom of the canoe is formed by bent frames with their ends stuck through slots cut 9 inches apart in the stringers.

The Irish canoes have ugly straight sides, because their stringers are cut out of imported deals. You may be able to find a piece of wood that will cut to a nice curve, which simplifies the work considerably, but more probably you will not. You may be able to bend a piece of elm to the right shape with hot water and fire, but it will take time, both to soften and to dry and set hard again, for it must be of fairly stout scantling, say 1¼-in. by 1¾-in; the foundation must be quite rigid before you start to build on it. When the piece is softened, bend it round a row of stout nails driven into the bench or floor, see that it is lying flat on the bench, and leave it for a day to set. Then split it with a fine saw, and you will have two stringers 1¼-in. wide and a little over ¾-in. deep, which should be identical. Assemble them at once, or they may lose their shape; don't start cutting the slots in them till the foundation is complete.

Another method is to build up the stringers in three thicknesses nailed together, the middle part of the sandwich being in short lengths with gaps between to form the slots for the frames. This is not so simple as it sounds. Amidships and aft, the parts of the sandwich have a rectangular section, and will stay put together as you bend them round the rows of nails; but forward, where the curve is sharper, the slots have to be formed with an increasing bevel to take the more V-shaped bow frames. That means all the parts have to be bevelled, and when bent they have a tendency to cant and slip sideways on each other. The nails they are bent round must be inclined, and they must be held down flat by pieces of wood screwed over them to the bench, till they are properly clenched together with copper through fastenings, two to each interval between the slots. A stringer so built up of deal will be as stiff as a solid one of elm.

The stringers are now fastened to the breast hook and transom and the thwarts fastened down to them to keep them to the right curve. The transom should have a good round to it, and, if the run of the grain suits, it may not need knees to connect it with the stringers. Leave the fore ends of the stringers a bit long on the breast-hook, so that they almost touch; then when the foundation is trued up, you can cut the notch for the stem accurately in them with a tenon saw. Now, if the stringers are solid, you cut the slots for the frames in them, ⅜-in. wide and ⅜-in.

in from the outside, and 1 inch long; but they need not be cut with great accuracy, because the frames have to move pretty freely in them, and it is convenient to be able to use small wedges.

The foundation is next turned upside down on two trestles, and the oak or elm stem fitted. At and above the breast-hook it may be quite light — say one-inch sided — and left square; below it expands, for about eighteen ribbands converge on it, it must be rabbeted to house their ends, and it has to hold a large number of nails. It is fitted in the notch cut for it and fastened to the breast-hook.

As in the boat described in the previous chapter, do not finish the lower end of the stem till you are ready to fit the ribbands to it. Similarly leave the aft side of the transom. It looks impossible that the ribbands could ever come fair on it, but they do. They leave rather an angle at each quarter, but that is no harm, for a tuck in the canvas skin starts just there. The frames, of elm, ash, or larch, should be an easy fit in the slots in the stringers, where they are not fastened till all the ribbands are on, except the midship frame and that furthest aft. Those must be steamed and set to the right shape inside a row of nails driven into a board — don't try to bend them outside the nails, or you will not get the curve true and you may break them. The after frame must be a specially strong one, for the ribbands make a sharp bend over it. Wedge and nail these two in their slots at the correct height and angle. The other frames may be bent approximately by hand as they are inserted; if they are fresh cut from a young and springy tree they will not need steaming, except those right forward, which are hard to get in because of the bevel. Their ends should stick far enough through the stringer to carry the gunwale.

Now comes the keel-plank, or central ribband. Before it is fitted, the ends of the foundation must be firmly lashed down to the floor, or they will be lifted by bending the keel-plank over the frames. I make the elm keel-plank some 3 inches wide from amidships aft, and rather thicker amidships than the other ribbands, but plane it down to a quarter of an inch where it passes over the after frame and the transom, for it has to be bent through nearly a right angle in a short distance there. The fore end is tapered to fit the stem. Soften the after end with hot water and fire, fix it about a foot below the transom, and lower the forward end gradually — if you have not enough headroom in your building shed for this you must bend the after end by hand first — till it lies in a fair curve over transom, after, and

midship frames, and the toe of the stem. (Push the other frames down out of the way, if they interfere with it.) Cut the fore end the right length to fit the stem, and fasten the keel-plank at those four points. Now push the other frames up till they touch it, and fasten them to it all along.

The rest of the ribbands may be 1½-in. wide amidships, tapered to ½-in. at each end; make the after taper a good long one, for some of the ends have to be sprung sideways considerably to fit on the transom, and they would cant if made too wide. They should be ⅜-in. thick, duced aft like the keel-plank. The ends may be softened with hot water and shaped roughly over the after frame, but the fastening must be started from forward. They will come quite close together forward, may be an inch apart amidships, and converge again on the transom, where they must be fitted together as well as may be and cut off short. It is easier to judge by eye of the symmetry of this openwork than of close planking, and a little adjustment of ribbands and frames will produce a smooth bottom with fair curves every way. When satisfied with it wedge and nail all the frames in their slots. A pair of raking half-frames can now be bent in between the stringers and the toe of the stem to strengthen the bluff of the bows. Since the ribbands run in a curve and the foundation stringers—which they cannot cross, because they have just the same projection outside the frames—are straight, there will be a space between them amidships, which must be filled with a stealer. The after ends of the ribbands are nailed outside the transom, which is not rabbeted for them, so they must be smoothed off and any spaces between them filled to avoid puckering the canvas covering. Then the bottom of the boat is complete as far as the foundation, and quite rigid, and she is turned right way up to fit the gunwales and finish the rest of the carpenter's work.

There are now standing up above the foundation the stem, the end of the keel-plank, and all the frames, but nothing at the quarters, where upright knees will have to be fixed to carry the ends of the gunwales and of the taffrail which connects them across the stern. The tops of the knees must be recessed half an inch on the outer and aft sides, so that the gunwales and taffrail, 1½-in. by ½-in. lie flush with them. The gunwales must be double, one part outside and one inside the frames, fastened together through them; a fastening to the frame only, so near the end of it, would not hold; but the taffrail, which goes outside the turned-up end of the keel-plank, can be single. The gunwales are connected to the stem with a breast-hook, but need no quarter-knees; they should, however, be stiffened by knees to the thwarts, which must be so arranged that the knee comes on a frame and is fastened to it. The inwale, or inner member of the gunwale, can then be considerably lighter than the outer one, and there is another piece going on outside that, so the whole will be quite stiff enough to stand the strain of rowing. Note that the filling pieces and lower chocks for the rowlocks, and any other fittings which need through fastenings, must be finished now, before the canvassing is begun. There are no ribbands between the foundation and the gunwale, but the wide gap between the stem and the first frame may be divided by a stancheon tenoned into the stringer. Turn the skeleton upside down again, and it is ready to have the skin put on.

The best material for this is a loosely woven hemp or flax canvas, which is softer and more easily stretched than cotton. It is obtained in 26-inch width, and three or four whole cloths can be put on amidships, stretching from gunwale to gunwale, but it must be halved to fit over the rounded ends. The first half-cloth should cover, from the taffrail down, all the transom, a bit of the round stern below the transom, and a bit of the sides above the stringer. Put it on with the selvage down, haul that edge taut and pin to the gunwale. At the angle between transom and gunwale there will be a dog's-ear of canvas sticking out, but disregard this for the present. The next half-cloth goes on with its selvage aft; pull it taut over the gunwales, but leave it as slack as you can along their length without showing wrinkles. Then carry on with whole cloths, well stretched fore and aft along the keel-plank and tacked to it, but slack along the gunwale, till you get into difficulties at the bows, where half-cloths will be wanted again. To finish, two triangular pieces must be sewn together with a curved seam to fit over the forefoot and stem.

However tight they may be pulled by hand the cloths will still have the after selvages slack and sticking out, but they can be shrunk into shape by a thorough soaking with water. Before doing this, see that they are very firmly tacked to the gunwales and keel-plank. When they are dry they will be slack again, but slack all over. Detach from the gunwale and haul taut, one at a time starting from aft, and tack down again. The skin will be much smoother, though the selvages will still stick out a little. Stitch them down to the cloth below at every 6 inches or so, through the spaces between the ribbands, to prevent their shifting, and put a couple of stitches in the dog's-ears at the quarters, and then you can take the whole skin off the framework and sew down the selvages all along; the sewing will tighten them so that they will lie quite flat when the skin is replaced. The other edges of the cloths, which will be kept tightly pressed against the ribbands, can be trimmed off roughly. Now stretch the skin over the frame again, and tack it to the gunwales, beginning from forward, and get a final pull on the dog's-ears at the quarters as you fold them in and tack them all long to the knees. Run a half-round fillet ¾-in. wide outside gunwales and canvas, and on the taffrail, and nail to them at short intervals; trim off the edge of the canvas to it, and the job is ready for painting or tarring, as preferred.

Only the outside is painted, as one cannot be sure of getting the paint in between the ribbands and the skin, nor of their sticking together, and water getting in there would not dry out, but rot the canvas. Tar is messy, but has the advantage that a small hole can be patched with a bit of rag and a hot iron. Sewing on a patch is rather troublesome. The stitches cannot be replaced by tacks in the ribbands, because no part of the skin is fixed to the framework, so any local tacking would be sure to tear away; they must be forced apart enough to make it possible to sew all round the patch. For this a useful tool is sold under the name of 'speedy stitcher'; it is an awl with an eye in the end like the needle of a sewing-machine, which shoves a bight of thread through the canvas; you pass another thread through that bight and pull it back, making a lock-stitch effect. Straining the canvas to get space under it for even this will make rather a blister on the skin, but it will soon smooth out.

A ten-foot canoe, built as I have described, would weigh about 70 pounds, and would stand quite a lot of rough usage. Canvas and paint account for a good deal of that weight, and a boat that was going to be carefully treated could save by using a thinner material for the skin, as well as by lighter scantlings in the frame. The sizes I mentioned gave me a useful knockabout craft lighter than I could have got by other means. I have been asked why, seeing that both the framing and the canvassing of the stern were the most difficult parts, I did not give her a flat board transom, like a pram. Well, I think the round stern made her pull easier and handle better than a pram, but, anyway, in a country where canoes are known one hesitates to build them in the wrong way. If I were building in England I might be tempted by the soft option.

VIII

SUNDRY FITTINGS

FITTINGS OF VARIOUS KINDS ARE NEEDED to finish the boat as it comes off the building stocks, and to equip it for its particular work. All boats must have an attachment for the painter and mooring rope; this, in an open boat, is a large ring-bolt inside the stem, and the rope passes over the gunwale, where, with nothing to prevent it from shifting sideways, it is exposed to chafe. The mooring rope is easily protected; make fast to the ring, and put a turn over the end of the stem, which generally stands up an inch or two above the gunwale, taking care that the part from the ring to the stem-head, where it makes the upper part of the turn, is taut; and there can be no shifting, and so no chafe. But a painter made fast to a larger vessel, or to a quay wall, might be pulled up off the stem-head, so if the boat is habitually tied up in this way, join it to the inside ring-bolt by a bit of chain just long enough to go over the gunwale. Of course the breast-hook and the gunwale must be protected by a strip of metal or stout leather, or the chain will cut them. It is very convenient to keep two painters always bent on, a stout one about 6 feet long with a large hook on the end, and a lighter one whose length will be dictated by the kind of place the boat is used in; if there is a big range of tide it should be very long. It is not the same thing to carry a spare long rope in the boat; that would probably be missing when most wanted. The long painter can be quite light; the boat will never break it, for its elasticity saves it from the shocks that break a short rope.

In a half-decked boat, where the stem-head does not usually make a convenient bollard, the mooring line passes through a fair-lead on the bow and is made fast to a cleat screwed to the deck some way abaft that, or, if as is often the case the cleat is not big enough -to take a decent-sized rope, to the mast. The rope cannot shift sideways in the fairlead, but the inboard part of it can stretch, and so allow chafe there; the rope should be parcelled in the way of the fair-lead with a strip of canvas wound round it and lashed firmly. This precaution will more often than not be forgotten, so it is better every way to have a length of chain reaching outside the fair-lead, which, being of metal, cannot be damaged by it, and bend the line to that. In the West Country they have a large hook on the end of the chain, and drop an eye on the mooring rope over that, thus keeping all the possibly muddy rope outboard (Fig. XIIA).

If the boat is to be towed at sea, or if she is large and heavy and has to be hauled up a beach with a tackle, you cannot pull her with her own painter, for you want the point of attachment as low down as possible. The best attachment is made to a thwartships hole in the stem or the fore end of the keel. You can tow from a large shackle with its pin through the hole; if the pin is screwed in the shackle it will work loose unless it has a lock-nut. It will also work loose in the hole, and cut through the wood unless that is protected; the best plan is to put two side plates over the scarf between stem and keel, well fastened to both, and drill the hole for the pin through them.

In most open boats the mast passes through a hole in a thwart and is stepped in a shallow box fastened either to a false kelson, the longitudinal plank serving to hold down the floor-boards, or, because the false kelson is movable and so may be accidentally displaced, to the keel or hog-stave. To step it, you have to lift it vertically above the thwart, and then lower it vertically, no easy jobs if the mast is a long one and the boat a bit lively. If she gives a lurch after the mast is entered in the hole it is liable to split the thwart, and even when its heel is right down it may have missed the step, which is invisible to the operator. A mast which has to be stepped and lowered at sea, as should be possible in all open boats, should be clamped in a half-round notch cut in the edge of the thwart, not passed through it.

A mast is naturally lowered and boated with its head aft, so it is clamped to the after side of the thwart. You have only to enter the heel in the step and lift the masthead, and the higher it is raised the easier the lift becomes. But till it is raised nearly upright the heel may slip out of a shallow step, so the fore side of the step must be made high enough to butt it against, or better, built up as a tabernacle or shallow trough fastened to the under side of the thwart and helping to support that. Or the mast may be clamped to the fore side of the thwart with the neat device used by the whale-boats in the Azores (Fig. VIIA). The clamp is a complete band hinged to turn up on the thwart, and the mast has a collar to prevent its passing too far through the clamp. Its heel is guided by a trough, the bottom of which is raised a couple of inches above the bottom of the step. As the mast comes towards the vertical, its heel is lifted by sliding along the bottom of the trough, till it is plumb, when it drops 2 inches into the step, and is held there without any pins or stays; to unstep it, it is lifted 2 inches, and it can be lowered without any danger of taking charge.

Dismasting is too often due to chain-plates coming adrift. A chain-plate, as you buy it, is a flat piece of iron with a big eye at the top for the shroud lanyard and two or three holes in the lower part to screw to the sheer-strake. This lower part cannot be longer than the width of the strake, while the eye may have a considerable projection above the gunwale. The shroud makes an angle of some 75 degrees with the vertical plate; the leverage tending to pull the lower part of the plate off the strake is small, but the strain is continuous, and it is increased now and then by blows on the eye as the boat bumps against a wall, for the eye of the plate—or rather the turns of the lanyard or the nut of the rigging screw in it—projects beyond the rest of the boat's structure. The holding power of the plate is great, as long as it is gripped tightly to the sheerstrake, but once it gets a shake most of its hold is gone. The chain-plate should be made with its eye bent well inboard, but since that is not a stock pattern, it is better to get it made like those of a big vessel (Fig. VIIID). The shackle needed with this pattern is by no means otiose. Shrouds are never bar-taut; as they swing about they bend, especially at their connexion with the chain-plate. If that connexion is between a hemp lanyard and a metal eye the hemp soon cuts; if it is between the pin of a shackle and the eye the lanyard does not shift on the bow of the shackle and so does not cut.

If the mast is habitually lowered the halyards are often regarded as sufficient staying for it; then they should be belayed as near the gunwale as possible. The strongest and handiest job is a long pin stuck horizontally through both thwart knees (Fig. XG). It can be left there permanently, for it is in the least likely place for people to catch their clothes on. Similar pins in the after thwart knees are for this reason better than cleats on the gunwale for the jib sheets. Halyards coming down by the mast are belayed on pins stuck through the thwart. These should not be ordinary belaying pins, which must by removed every time the mast is lowered, or someone may sit on them, but round-headed bolts flush with the thwart, which can be left there. If you pass the halyard under the pin and jam the bight between the edge of the thwart and its own part it should hold safely and can be freed in an instant; or take the bight forward over the thwart, back under it, and jam as before for extra security.

Thwarts, other than the mast thwart, commonly have a little stanchion fitting into slots under them and in the bottom board. If one is missing replace it; it was not put there to hold down the bottom boards but to hold up the thwart if a heavy man sat on it.

The common crutch-shaped rowlocks fit iron sockets in the gunwales, or sometimes only brass or iron plates screwed down to them, but they don't stay a fit very long unless the ends of the shanks are kept from moving by chocks 2 or 3 inches below the gunwale. Rowlocks are not all the same length; see that you haven't any too short to reach the chocks. They generally have a small hole in the end of the shank. I have no idea what this hole was designed for, but I know that it must not be used for a lanyard. If it is, it takes two hands to ship the rowlock, with the result that either it is left permanently shipped till it comes into collision with something and splits the gunwale, or the lanyard is cut off and the rowlock lost. Make the lanyard fast round the neck of the crutch, above the gunwale, securing the end midway between the forward and after sockets, so that a man wanting to shift his rowing position has no excuse for casting it loose.

A stretcher in the right place adds to the rower's efficiency and also to the comfort of his backside, always a sore subject to the unpractised oar. Do not trust to any bit of stick propped against a frame; its ends will chafe the plank where they rest on it; it should fit a notched piece of wood screwed to the bottom boards or bilge stringer. When it is possible for any item of boat's gear to serve two purposes it should do so. The ends of the stretcher must be shaped to fit the notches, but the middle part may be any shape; make it such that it serves as a skid for hauling up the boat on, with one wide flat side and the other half-round. A bit of a 4-in. spar sawn down the centre makes two good stretchers.

When a boat is built with a centreboard the keel and hog-stave are made wide enough to take the fastenings needed to hold the case down to them, but an old boat may have a narrow keel and no hog-stave (Fig. IID). The only practicable way of making a water-tight joint is to heave down the case tight on to the hog-stave by bolts through a hard-wood batten fixed near the bottom of the case; but if the bolts come outside the hog-stave or too near the edge of it there is nothing else to heave them down to. You cannot pull on the garboards, or you would merely split the edge off—that is the weakest point in the whole boat—and you have cut out the only fastenings of the frames, which were in the centre of the keel. Screw two side-pieces, a little longer than the slot, to the keel, outside—they will probably be wanted anyway, for strength—and heave down the case to them, putting a strip of cloth soaked in thick paint between it and the hog-stave. Since the frames must be left with some bearing on the hog-stave the bottom edge of the case must be very narrow, and the top of the hog-stave may not be very true and smooth, so they must be hove together really hard to keep the water out; it would be an endless job to notch the batten on the case to fit accurately half a dozen frames, which may not be of even thickness, so it is better to leave a bit of clearance over the frames and tighten them down with wedges after the case is secured in place.

Since there is a considerable sideways strain on the case, especially at its fore end, the posts which form its ends should have projections going down through the slot the whole depth of the keel, and they should be planned so that they are fastened to thwarts fore and aft. A continuous obstruction the height of the thwarts is no more likely to trip you up than a lower one whose ends are not conspicuous. But the best way to deal with an old boat is to use a dagger plate, the shorter slot of which need only cut two or three frames.

One sometimes sees centreboards hung in a way which may lead to serious trouble, viz. with their pivots through the case below the waterline, or even through an external keel. It should be possible to lift the plate out while the boat is afloat; moreover, the plate should have a good deep housing in the case when it is down, or the strain of a lever some 4 feet long below its fulcrum and only a few inches above it must sooner or later split the keel or start leaks in the case. The plate has two main forms; the old style is generally hung from a pivot through its forward bottom corner—lower than it ought to be—and lifted by a handle attached to its after corner. But it can be hung from its upper corner, if that is made triangular (Fig. VIIB). It may not hang quite vertical when it is down, but it has a bearing on the whole depth of the case, and it is easily accessible. In the new style (Fig. VIIc) the pivot is low down, and the lifting is done by pulling the upper forward corner of the plate forward with a wire or chain. If that corner is made square you have something worse than a three to one leverage against you when lifting—the plate may not weigh much, but if a small stone or a lump of mud has got into the case you have not power enough to shift it—so there generally is a horn extending forward from it to increase the purchase. If the horn is not to stand above the top of the casing when the plate is right up, the front of the casing must be cut down enough to house it—whether this is undesirable depends on the height of the case above the waterline. Usually the pivot does not go through a hole in the plate but in a notch cut slantwise in it, so the plate can be removed by a straight-up lift without taking out the pivot. Note that when raising the plate with its tackle in the ordinary course it is not bearing on the pivot but against the fore end of the case; so see that there is not too much clearance between them or you will pull the plate off the pivot. There should be some way of locking the plate when up, in case the tackle is let go by accident; a clip over the horn or a pin through case and plate at that end of it.

To lift a heavy plate hung in this way you want a powerful tackle, which is out of place in a boat's bottom. I much prefer the differential used in racing dinghies; it is merely two drums of different sizes mounted on the same spindle; the lifting wire is wound on the small one, and the rope you haul on the reverse way on the other. There is no difficulty about lifting the old style plate. You have a straight pull, just the way a weight-lifter likes it, on its after end. Commonly the handle is on an iron bar, so you can pull and push the plate up and down with it to clean out the case, but when the plate is up, the bar is rather an obstruction in the boat, even if it is jointed. As long as the boat is always kept afloat a chain or wire could be substituted. The bar, chain, or wire, is of course a slight obstruction to sailing too, but in spite of that I prefer this plate to the new style for a working boat because of its simplicity. To unship the plate its fore end must be held up while the pivot is taken out; this can be done by slipping a loop of seizing wire into a notch cut in the plate close under the pivot-hole. Then the plate can be lifted out of the aft end of the case by the handle, or if there is a thwart in the way there, the handle can be removed and the plate lifted out forward by the wire loop. I have perhaps made rather too good a case for this type of centreboard by showing in my drawing the lifting handle short enough to fold down between two thwarts; more often the arrangement of the thwarts would require it to come abaft the after one, and to be 3 or 4 feet long, making it more difficult to lift as well as to stow, for one man

can hardly hold it up while he stoops down to put the locking pin in the plate. If
the lifting bar is close enough to a thwart you can hold it up by bending the handle
down over the thwart; if not, cut a notch in the bar, to engage on a pin through the
upper part of the case, while you get down to lift the last few inches and insert the
locking pin.

I do not think a centreboard should be regarded as ballast; I would make it as
light as is consistent with stiffness. You may want to get it up when the pressure
of sailing is on it, to float over an obstruction or to ease the boat in a squall—she is
not so likely to capsize when the plate is up and she can blow sideways.

For a small job I favour the dagger plate rather than the centreboard. It is simply a parallel-sided plate dropped vertically through a slot in the keel. The slot
and the casing therefore need only be as long as the width of the plate, or about
a third of the length of the centreboard casing. Personally I make the case longer
than that so that I can shift the plate a little fore and aft to correct the boat's form;
also to make it easier to get out if I should run aground. And it is obviously the
right instrument to use to clear the slot of mud and stones, if the boat is used on a
beach where she picks up such things. But really sticky mud, which squeezes up
till it fills the casing and hardens there, is not easy to shove out even with a dag-
ger-plate; where that is likely to happen I suggest, as a cleaner alternative to any
device needing an opening in the boat's bottom, a lee-board hung over her side.

A small leeboard is very easy to make and to handle, and does not involve any
structural alterations to the boat, if her gunwale is strong enough. As Fig. VIID
shows, it is hooked over the gunwale and kept vertical by a chock of wood on it
which presses against the boat's side about a foot down. While it is to leeward it
cannot possibly shift, but when the pressure is relaxed it floats away from the side
and can be lifted inboard and passed over to the other side. The difficulty with
this simple form is that if you want to lift it while the boat is sailing, you can't. The
supporting chock, which cannot be omitted in a boat of normal shape, or her gunwale would be torn off, catches under the lands of the planks or rubbing strake.
An emergency release for the hook or clip over the gunwale should be arranged; it
might be combined with the lifting handle, as figured. Personally I find it easier to
lift the board by a handle fixed horizontally on the outside, and some way down it;
but a handle gets broken if you can't unship the board in a hurry when rounding

up alongside a quay or a big vessel. The board should be as light as possible, if it is to be passed across the boat with one hand when making tacks. It should be flat or slightly concave on the outer or pressure side, and convex on the inside, and it will lift the boat to windward like the wing of an aeroplane. As it will be shipped forward of amidships, where the boat's sides begin to converge to the bows, the slight angle will give it a further lift to windward; for its size it is more effective than a centreboard.

Another way of fitting a leeboard, mechanically good, but involving some gear inside the boat, is this. Support it on the gunwale merely by a peg, not a hook, prolong it up 6 or 8 inches, and fix a chain or wire of the right length to this prolongation and to a point on the centre line of the boat—best on a thwart, if there happens to be one in the right place. The tautness of the chain and its height above the gunwale will prevent the board from being forced under the boat without any need for the chock or distance piece against her side, which is rather an obstruction to her sailing. The chain will hold the board in place equally well on either side of her, if care is taken not to put turns in it when tacking. The quick release slip would be at the attachment of the chain to the thwart or kelson.

Large pivoted leeboards, such as are used by barges and Dutchmen, are only practicable on a barge type of craft, with perfectly flat sides or with a projecting strake near the waterline to keep the boards off a curved side; without these conditions it would be impossible to move them up or down on a pivot.

The ordinary boat's mainsail sets better at all times the farther off the centreline it can be sheeted; the main-sheet block therefore travels across the stern on a horizontal iron bar or 'horse'. When the sail is a boomless one the sheet-block may not stay put at the end of a straight horse, but a little kink forward in the bar there will hold it. The horse is rather a nuisance for a knockabout or working boat, apt to get bent if you use her for carrying long, awkward loads, and preventing the shipping of a steering or sculling oar. There is much to be said for omitting it in the case of a boomless sail, and working the sheet on a pin in the transom or quarter-knee, as will be explained in detail in the next chapter. The whole question of handling the tiller and the sheet by one man in a small boat is a difficult one, involving the most convenient steering position for the man, and the length of the tiller. He has to get round the tiller, keeping control of it, while he holds the sheet in his hand, and avoid being pitched overboard while doing so. Undoubtedly his easiest way of getting round is to slide across the after thwart on his backside, facing aft, using a tiller long enough to be within his reach all the time. But there should also be a short tiller in the boat, as he may have to sit right aft if he has passengers aboard. A tiller should be easy to make, if you want to carry a selection of them, but it is not always so. Sometimes the tiller is made with a slot in it, to ship over a straight rudder-head. That is uneconomical. The slot should be in the rudder, which is much less likely to get lost or broken, or otherwise need replacement or duplication, and then any bit of stick will serve for a tiller.

The rudder may not get broken, but when, as in most sailing boats, it extends some little way below the keel, it often breaks the lower pintle, the pin on the stern-post to which it is hung. If the rudder can quite easily be raised a foot or so—which, by the way, involves unshipping the tiller if there is a main-sheet horse above it—and lowered again when an obstruction is passed, the raising will not be left dangerously late. But the hanging of many rudders is perversely awkward; you can unship them easily enough, but the upper and lower pintles are made exactly the same length, so that they have to be entered in their respective gudgeons simultaneously, which is almost impossible in a lop of sea. I suggest a way of making the job quite easy (Fig. VIIE). It is not perfect, for the rudder can only be lifted, with the certainty of dropping back into place again, by the height of the transom above the upper gudgeon, which one is tempted to put too low for strength, but I think it is the most practical solution of the problem that I have seen. To prevent the possibility of the pintle being knocked out of the hook fitting and bent when the rudder is unshipped a ring can be slipped over it down on the hook. The pintle could not be made very stiff, for it has to be sprung sideways out of the hook to let the lower rudder gudgeon pass, but it would have no need to be, for it is supported at two places at all material times.

IX

RIGGING AND RUNNING GEAR

SAILS ARE PUT IN A BOAT SO THAT A SINGLE MAN can navigate her if she is too heavy for a pair of paddles; they defeat their own end therefore if he cannot safely handle them alone. He can set a sail after a fashion with any sort of gear, and enough expenditure of time and labour, but to take it in smartly it must be rigged exactly right. One sees purchases in which the theoretical gain of power is reduced by a half by the friction of stiff rope in many small and bad blocks, but, as few of the hoists in a boat really require a purchase at all, this is immaterial; the sail goes up, if slowly. But the same friction doubles its resistance to lowering, and gravity alone will not bring it down; the single man has to leave the helm, and go forward and haul down the flapping canvas by hand, with the chance of stepping into a coil of unnecessary rope on the way and fouling it for running. Every extra fathom of rope and every extra block is a potential danger. One large block weighs less and costs less than two small ones; and if it looks less yachty, which I dispute, the motto of the boat-sailor should be safety first.

All text-books assume that sails can only be taken in when the boat is head to wind, and most boats appear to be rigged on that assumption, which is a very dangerous one. Suppose your boat, running free with all sail set, is overtaken by a prolonged squall or strikes an unexpected patch of rough water, you can ease her by putting her straight before the wind; but you can't carry all sail indefinitely on that course, and if you try to round her up, as the books advise, before you have reduced sail drastically, she will certainly capsize. No one should go alone in an open boat unless he can lower, close-reef, or effectually scandalize his mainsail instantly and without fail on any course, especially before the wind, without leaving the tiller; and the simpler the gear is the more likely is this to be possible.

In a small boat often worked with oars it must be easy to lower the mast and boat the spars out of the way of the rowers, so there will be no stay or shrouds, and up to a length of 15 feet and a beam of 5 one sail will be enough. It is generally a standing lug or a spritsail. I prefer the lug, because with the balance-reef fitting described on p. 43 and Fig. IIIA it is really safe. It is not so easy to get a sprit down;

if, as is usual, its heel is supported by being jammed in the snotter it takes two hands to get it out. I suggest that the snotter be formed of two rope grommets, one a tight fit on the mast and the other a slack fit on the sprit, and kept well greased, the sprit being held up only by the heel-rope from the masthead. When this is let go, the heel of the sprit would fly forward through the snotter and the peak come down—perhaps. The snotter would have a tendency to ride up the mast, and a small cleat would be wanted to keep it down. This heel-rope, like the halyard of the lugsail, should lead through a block at the foot of the mast and be belayed within the helmsman's reach. A small boat is better without a boom on her mainsail; if there is one, it must be capable of being topped right up to the mast by a reliable topping-lift. Many accidents occur through a boom or the loose canvas of a sail as it is lowered falling foul of the helmsman at a critical moment.

I have described in Chapter V how a boomless sail is sheeted to a horse, but a horse is often undesirable. In its absence the sheet block should have a longish strop of stiff rope to hang it over a pin projecting aft through the transom. Don't omit the block and catch the rope itself on the pin, as fishermen often do; you can't trim the sail, you soon cut the rope, and you are more likely to get the rope crossed when shifting it than if you had a block to handle. The operation is so easy that I have no desire to ship a horse, though I have to handle a leeboard as well as the sheet.

A single-part sheet will do for a sail up to 70 or 80 square feet area, but at that size holding it for any length of time is very hard on the hand, and there should be a block on the clew of the sail, the standing end of the sheet being made fast to the lead-block. For comfort the rope must be fairly thick, but the block on the clew of the sail may be smaller than I should allow anywhere else; the trouble is not hauling the sheet in but holding it, so this is the one place where friction helps. If you don't mind wearing out the rope pretty quickly don't use a block there at all, but reeve it through the clew cringle, and there will be nothing heavy to hit you on the head.

The lug and sprit are the commonest rigs for a working boat because the spars can be detached at once from the mast; the gaff and what I call the gunter-sprit, to be described later, are only suitable if their spars can be triced up to the mast and the sail brailed to it, to avoid interference with the working, and that makes the mast heavier and the gear more complicated. I want to make a plea for treating the simplest possible things with respect. Many amateurs refuse to recognize such craft as sailing boats, just because they are not written up in the yachting press. They are cheap, but not necessarily nasty. A well-thought-out rig over a good hull may be highly efficient for its particular service. We are more likely to improve on the age-old practice of watermen and fishing boats by independent thinking than by borrowings from racing dinghies.

To turn to boats specifically designed for sailing, whose masts are usually kept standing, supported by wire shrouds and stays. If the mast is a long one the staying must be really good; nowadays few anchorages are always calm, for those most sheltered from wind and sea are most exposed to the wash of motor-boats. A boat is subject to as much wear and tear while on moorings as when sailing, and spends very much more time there; so unless her rigging is so simple that her mast not only can be, but actually is, unstepped at night it must hold the mast firmly enough to prevent her structure being racked and battered when she rolls or pitches. And, since even wire rigging stretches, the mast should be wedged tight in the deck, clamp, or thwart that supports it.

The rigging of a racing mast is an expert's job, which I am not dealing with in this book. I assume that a forestay and one shroud a side, and no backstays, will hold up any ordinary boat's mast. The weight and windage of this small quantity of wire are insignificant, and there is no need to make it of extreme thinness, nor of high-tensile steel, which is particularly liable to rust. Many boats are rigged with wire no more than $\frac{1}{8}$-in. in diameter. This may have a breaking strain of half a ton, when new, but unless it is very carefully treated it will not retain that strength long. The wire, described as 6 × 7, consists of six strands with seven wires in each, laid up round a hemp heart; it is hard to conceive the thinness of the coating of zinc on the forty-two individual wires which keeps them from rust, but it is easy to realize how little wear and corrosion will remove that coating. Zinc by itself corrodes pretty rapidly in salt water, but in contact with iron, to which it is electro-positive, it goes very quickly indeed. You will see the lower ends of shrouds a mass of rust while the rest is quite good. And, unless great care is taken to make the serving over a splice watertight, rust will start where the marling-spike has damaged the zinc coating.

Of course a shroud made of seven wires only, six laid up round a central one, would be not only stronger but seven times as durable. This construction may be seen in use in a variety of sizes as stays for telegraph poles, fences, and seizing wire; but all these are iron wires with a tensile strength only a quarter of that of plough steel, which is usually specified. If 7×1 steel wire is made I have never seen it. You can get 19×1, that is, the whole nineteen wires laid up together, not in separate strands, with a breaking strain of a ton for a diameter of ⅛-in., but not, I fancy, galvanized; I have never seen this small stuff in use. Or single wires, still stronger. I have seen these, well coated either with varnish or with rust, so I presume they are not procurable galvanized. But these prodigious figures for breaking strains are no business of ours; let us halve our initial requirements, with the knowledge that our rigging will be just as strong in five years' time, and use iron fencing wire, either 7×1, making it twice as heavy and one and a half times as thick, or a single wire, the same weight, but rather thinner for the strength. It is bad policy to make a rope or a rod subject to mechanical or chemical loss unnecessarily thin. Its strength increases in duplicate ratio with its diameter, but its surface in simple ratio; for example, a ¼-inch wire is four times as strong as an ⅛-inch, but is only twice as much attacked by rust. And the same applies to the wear on a hemp rope.

A common splice in 7×1 iron wire is not sound. I made one on a short test piece with a Post Office splice—a modification of that used on the stays of telegraph poles—on the other end. The wire broke at the last tuck of the common splice; the other was undamaged. I had no way of measuring how much more load was needed to break that, so I cannot recommend the Post Office splice, which is a clumsy job anyway. Splices in rigging wire give only 85 per cent. of its strength, and are quite out of date. A 100 per cent. strong connexion is made by soldering the end of the wire into a coned socket (Fig. VIIc), if this is obtainable in the size wanted; or by making a round turn on a small thimble and seizing the end back to its standing part, if the thimble can be prevented from turning by keying it to the shackle which holds it (Fig. VIIId).

The rigging of a boat's mast which has to stow inboard is often shackled aloft to a band with eyes on it, to shorten the spar, instead of being made with long eyes to go over the masthead. The band is liable to work loose in hot dry weather, crush the wood, and pull down; it should not be used except on a mast which is frequently lowered and under inspection. With a plain masthead, only the fore-stay need have an eye spliced in it. The shrouds can be in one piece, with a round turn on the masthead, the legs being seized to the turn so as to come opposite each other (Fig. VIIIA). Or make a clove hitch with them, with the hitch on the aft side of the masthead; the main halyards put a big wringing strain on the mast-head, and the tangential pull of the shrouds counteracts that. But see that they do not foul the peak halyards if you have a gaff sail. The throat of a spliced eye makes a funnel to lead water into the heart of the shroud, unless it is well protected. Put a seizing of several figure-of-eight turns of wire across the throat, and cover that with insulating tape or calico soaked in paint or tar before you serve over it; and use soft spun-yarn or stout sail-twine for the serving, not hard ' yacht marline', which does not stay put (Fig. VIIIB).

When the mast is stepped through or clamped to a thwart there is a good rea-son for placing the chain-plates right abreast of it, where the gunwale is stiffened by the thwart knees; but from here the shroud gives the mast no support against the pull of the jib, which consequently shows a sagging luff and does not draw properly. The shroud should lead at an angle of 30 degrees or so abaft the mast to be any use as a backstay; its interference with squaring off the boom when run-ning is more than offset by the increased efficiency of the jib when close-hauled. No boat is likely to set more than one headsail, so if she has a bowsprit the fore-stay will lead to the end of that, and a bobstay will be needed to hold it down. The bobstay should be of chain, since wire will not stand contact with salt water. As the bowsprit will probably not be more than a couple of feet outboard it is unnec-essary to make provision for running it in, and the bobstay may be cut to the right length and shackled on. The forestay has to be detached to unstep the mast, but there is no reason why its connexion too should not be made with a shackle. After the shroud lanyards have been let go the mast can easily be bent forward with the jib halyards enough to get the pin in and out of the shackle.

If the mast is to be lowered frequently the shroud lanyards should be of 9-thread hambro line, one end spliced to a triangular thimble on the shroud; three or four turns through this and the chain-plate will be enough. It looks best to fin-ish it off with a hitch round the shroud above the thimble, big-ship fashion, but it is commonly hitched below the thimble and the end wound round all its parts till it looks like a sausage. Hambro line is hard, stiff stuff, and must be well greased, but the lanyard cannot be prevented from shifting more or less on the thimble and plate, and a softer material would be cut. Where the mast is always left standing, however, use an ordinary thimble on the shroud and enough turns of soft tarred spunyarn to fill it and the eye of the chain-plate pretty tight, so that they stick together and to the metal and do not chafe. As a matter of fact I know more cases of chain-plates breaking or tearing off than of shrouds or lanyards parting, which is absurd.

If I condemn the 42 wires in steel standing rigging for lack of durability, still more do I condemn the 144 wires in 6×24 flexible running rigging. Leave that to the racing dinghy; the ordinary boat is not seriously handicapped by the quantity of 1¼-inch or 1½-inch manilla or hemp needed, which is very small if intelligently applied. To take the worst possible standing lug or a gaff-sail set in the Azorean way, the set of which is spoiled by the smallest stretch in their single tye halyard, three fathoms of 1½-inch tarred hemp, once it is well stretched, will not pull down any more in six hours' hard sailing, wet or fine; but, according as it is wet or fine, it will, equally with the wire halyard, want a lot of adjusting to the shrinking and stretching of the sail. To set a big mainsail—150 square feet is the limit I proposed in this book—with a single part of stiff rope would be hard work; one would need a whip on the tye halyard, calling for another 4 fathoms of 1¼-inch manilla. But only a few feet of that would be above the gunwale, adding to the air resistance of the tye. The saving effected by making the tye of wire is hardly worth considering.

When estimating the power needed to hoist a sail I am only considering lifting the weight of the sail itself and the gaff or yard it hangs from. The yard should be peaked, in the case of a lugsail, or the luff of a gaff-sail stretched, by the tack tackle; the weight of the boom, if any, taken by the topping lift. It is not an economy to omit these two inconsiderable items and multiply the power of the halyards to make them do three jobs instead of one. For years the up-to-date yachtsman has insisted that he couldn't use a tack tackle with a mainsail laced to the boom, but in the latest racing yachts he admits that coasters and fishermen knew better than he all the time. Let us be really up to date and copy the racing yacht rather than the unenlightened phase. I see no sense in lacing a boat's sail to the boom, except to allow of roller reefing, so we will roller-reef in the simplest and most effective way. Fit the boom with strong jaws instead of the usually ill-designed gooseneck; do not parrel them to the mast, like gaff jaws, for they will never come away from it till you want them to. To reef, pull the jaws away aft, roll up the boom by hand, and ship them back again. Now the tangential pull of the sail will put a twisting strain on the jaws, which will soon damage them and the mast, however well protected they are, so in attaching the tack tackle to the boom take it over the same side as the sail is on, and it will exactly neutralize that pull, and leave no more cause of chafe than when the whole sail was set. Of course the boom can go up the mast to any height, which is sometimes convenient to keep it out of the water when running before a big sea, or to give the helmsman a clear view all round if he is manoeuvring in a narrow space.

The topping lift does not need any block aloft; indeed, unless in the case of a boom which is topped up and down the mast to furl the sail, it does not need any block at all. Make fast to the masthead a line with a hook on it to engage with an eye on the boom and support that a little higher than its sailing position; when the sail is set unhook the lift and let the weight of the boom come on the sail. For roller reefing the eye must of course be on the swivelling fitting at the end of the boom; if you cannot reach that instead of the hook and eye the lift must be rove through a block there and led forward to be belayed on the mast. When reefing, belay it anywhere out of the way; the sail rolls up better if there is no weight on the lift. To top a boom right up the block must be similarly placed.

When speaking of the stretching of halyards I said nothing about keeping the wire luff-rope of a jib good and taut, because I see no reason for setting a jib with a lot of wire when you already have the forestay, the principal piece of wire in the ship, only an inch or two away, to hank it to. Setting a jib flying, that is, all adrift and full of wind with the sheets flying round your head, or hanging on to the buoy-rope of a mooring while the sheets again are committing assault and battery, are such nasty jobs that one sees even in quite small boats the jib wound up on a roller by gear hardly good enough for a window-blind; at any rate it often refuses to wind up if there is a breeze. I am distressed by the number of jibs I see left unprotected on their rollers by week-enders from Monday to Saturday, wet or fine, and I am disgusted by the appearance of those jibs on Sunday. Why they are left there when the mainsails are taken ashore to keep dry passes all understanding, unless it is to emphasize the fact that the roller jib is an unseamanlike device anyway. When you have at the most a couple of feet of bowsprit there is no excuse for it. A jib hanked to the forestay cannot possibly give trouble while it is being hoisted; when it is up there is no great weight on the halyards; it comes down quicker than a roller rolls up (if that does roll up) and cannot get adrift afterwards, provided that a downhaul is properly fitted; and you can unbend half a dozen spring hanks from the stay in less than a minute, and carry the sail away out of the rain. Why is the hanked jib not in universal use, as the hanked foresail is on yachts which have two headsails? Because one of the few economies practised on yachts is the omission of a fore downhaul. It may be safe enough to pull down the sail by hand in a big vessel with high bulwarks, but I have seen it very nearly end in a drowning accident in a small one. Bend the downhaul to the head cringle of the sail or to the halyards, reeve it down through all the hanks, and through a block on the bowsprit or stem head, make it long enough to reach a pin near the foot of the mast and always keep it fast there while under way, and you have a foolproof method of se-curing the jib. Note that if the stay is shackled to the bowsprit or stem there must be a large stop — a Turk's head or a toggle lashed on — at the top of the serving of the splice or the seizing to keep the hanks on the bare wire, for if they slip down over the serving they will jam there (Fig. VIIIE). The hanks should be good and big, they have to include the downhaul as well as the stay, and most spring hanks are a bad shape; too narrow, and apt to jam when twisted sideways by the folding of the luff-rope of the sail. A really satisfactory pattern, such as that illustrated in Fig. IXA, would have to be specially made, so a set of them might cost nearly as much as roller fittings; but they would soon pay for themselves by saving the depreciation of a roller jib.

GEAR AND GADGETS

JUST AS A MINIATURE YACHT MAKES A BAD SMALL BOAT, so models of her gear and fittings work badly on a much reduced scale, and are in fact unsafe. The fair sailing strains on them decrease as something like the fourth power of their linear dimension, so theoretically they could be made even smaller than they are; but, apart from the fact that it has to be used at sea in bad conditions by large and clumsy human hands, a very small part is liable to be broken by a very slight accident, and the structure of the material it is made of has to be taken into account. A small screw will not hold in soft wood with an open grain; a fine thread cut on an iron pin may strip, for iron also has a grain.

The most serious screw trouble is with Bermudan tracks. The best of these is bad, and the worst of them is commonest. If people, in spite of warnings and horrible examples, insist on using them because they are the fashion, let them be at least as good as their nature allows, even if it means a little more weight and bulk. I do not recommend holding the luff-rope of the sail in a groove worked on the mast, as some racing boats practise; wood and sail-twine do not form good bearing surfaces, however well greased they are, and a few hours' hard sailing on a wet day will strip the roping right off the sail and let it all go adrift. I am thinking of metal slides on a metal track. The track, of whatever form it is, has generally so little stiffness that it has to be closely fastened; now if any one of the dozens of small screws that hold it to the spar comes out an eighth of an inch it may hang up the whole train of slides, so little clearances have they. A stiffer track, not weakened by countersinking the screw-holes, would need fewer screws, and they could be larger, with round heads, if the slides were designed to clear them. The simplest form of slide is the one that comes down easiest, merely a half-hoop of round bar-iron passing loosely through the eyelet in the sail, and held to the track by lugs, for the sail can blow round it sideways and does not jam it. But it has three faults; it does not go up so easily, for gravity and friction cant it and press the luff-rope of the sail against the track; any lubricant soon washes off it; and as it comes off the track it must be taken out of the sail and put in your pocket, for it is essential to free working that it should not be seized on. A small addition cures these three faults (Fig. IXc). The lugs, instead of gripping the track itself, grip a box-slide an inch or so long which runs on the track; it runs more easily because of its long bearing, and it can be kept packed with grease. The hoop should be of such a size that it takes some twisting about and forcing to assemble the slide on the sail, so it will be very unlikely to come off; still, if the thing can be put together by any means at all it can also come adrift by accident when the sail is being carted about, so carry a couple of spares. A further precaution: it would not kill a boat, when she is not racing, to have a downhaul bent to the head of the sail; it is much easier to pull it down with a rope than by gripping the canvas, and the rope is handy, anyway, to secure the head when it is down.

Small blocks are a very false economy, for they are ruinous to ropes. You can buy blocks of a sort for sixpence, but they will chafe through many sixpenny-worths of rope, and may do worse, if a broken strand jams in the block and leads to a bad accident. Decent wooden blocks only cost a shilling, or you can buy the sheaves for threepence and make the shells yourself—if you like neatness you can make them much smaller than the bought ones for the same size of sheave. The size of sheaves and the stiffness of the rope between them govern the loss of power from friction in a tackle; see how much effort it takes to bend a stiff rope into a sharp curve; you are doing that all the time, and it can't do the rope any good. The loss from the friction of the sheave on its pin is comparatively small; it, and the wear on the pin, can be eliminated by using patent roller sheaves, but I do not recommend these for very small blocks. The rollers are all right, but they only leave room between them for a very thin pin which is liable to bend.

Fitting a sheave in a soft-wood spar needs care, especially the masthead halyard sheave, which carries a heavy and continuous weight. Unless the pin is a thick one it is liable to pull down through the wood, perhaps more on one side than on the other, when the sheave runs crooked, enlarges the hole in the mast, and may allow the halyard to ride off it and jam. A metal plate, bent in the shape of a long U, should line the hole, resting on the bottom of it, drilled for the pin, so as to take all the weight of that off the wood (Fig. IXe). Where there is only a light weight on a rope, where the rope is only used for a short time, or where, when in use, it does not move through the block, as in a jib downhaul, a topping lift, or a tack tackle, a lignum vitae bull's-eye or a wide brass thimble is better than a block, which may get displaced and so give the rope a foul lead. That does not matter with the bull's-eye, because it is rounded every way, and so does not cut the rope like the sharp edge of the cheek of the block.

A great deal of damage is done by blocks with strops which are too short and stiff, by swivel blocks whose swivels jam, and by hook blocks which are hooked on the wrong cant. They may appear to give the rope a fair lead before the sail is hoisted, but it may be a foul lead when the sail is right up; the rope may render all right on one tack but be cutting itself to pieces on the other. You can't see well from below if the blocks at the masthead are lying the right way, so make sure they will turn easily whatever way the rope wants to pull them. If they are hooked to eyebolts through the mast or eyes on a mast-band see that those eyes are turned in the direction of the worst strain; for instance, in a gaff-rigged boat, the eye for the throat halyards should be vertical and that for the peak horizontal. The hooks of most iron-stropped blocks are too small and of a bad shape; unless you have to save fractions of an inch in overall length use blocks with a loose hook, or make them up yourself with a rope strop. It seems to be difficult to buy a block with a loose hook, but not so hard to get one with a staple. Back the pin out, and you can withdraw the staple, put a suitable hook on this, and replace (Fig. XA). But, where possible, prefer a hemp grommet strop, the strength of which you know and the condition of which is open to view, to an internal iron strop, which is sometimes badly weakened by the hole for the pin bored through it. A grommet is made like the rope ring you play deck quoits with. Take a strand rather more than three times as long as the circumference of the grommet, and lay it up three-stranded, passing it through the eye of the hook, and finish off the ends as in a long splice. Seize the block in with the join of the strand in the score in the tail of the block, where it is quite hidden.

There is one block the fittings of which should be as compact and rigid as possible. Most patterns, when used for the main sheet travelling on an iron horse, have a way of falling over and getting foul, or losing the pins of their shackles. You cannot buy the pattern I want, but it is easy to make it. Buy a block with staple, as described for the hook-block, take out the staple with its rounded bow and replace it by a flat strap, the bow part a little wider than the diameter of the horse. Now any shackle wide enough in the jaws to go on the horse will be a nice fit on the bow of the strap, and when the pin is screwed up tight will be fixed there rigidly, especially if grooves are filed in the jaws of the shackle to fit the strap; the shackle will not stick on the horse and its pin will not come out (Fig. XB).

The horse is commonly a plain iron bar with its ends bent down through the quarter-knees and held there by nuts under them. To prevent the shackle of the sheet-block slipping over the bend and jamming Turk's heads are worked on the bar with a bit of marline. Unless the Turk's heads are much bigger than is usual the shackle must be smaller than will slide freely on the bar. A more effective and not too unsightly wooden stop could be devised. Make a little hard-wood stanchion an inch more than the diameter of the bar and an inch higher than the horse is above the quarter-knee, bore a hole down through it for the turned-down end of the bar, and cut a slot 1½ inch deep on one side for the horizontal part. The wood should be served with wire or leather above and below the bar to protect it from blows of the iron shackle (Fig. XC).

One sheave always has more or less of a foul lead, that is the one over which the main halyard passes through the mast. To limit the length of the mast one naturally wants to hoist the yard of a lug or sliding gunter as close as possible up to this sheave, and that prevents the yard from rotating round the mast in light winds and so spoils the set of the sail, and when a strong wind forces it to rotate puts a heavy strain on the gear. Rotating masts have been used in some small racing boats to avoid this stiffness, but they are hardly practical for us. A gaff can be rigged so as to avoid it. Put the throat halyard sheave right at the masthead, and there will be enough drift between that and the gaff jaws to allow them to work freely; and mount the peak halyard block on a long hemp strop swivelling round the pole of the mast clear above the other fittings. I have seen this strop made of wire, covered with leather, and I have seen such wire strops break from frequent bending—they are bent pretty sharply every time the sail is hoisted or lowered— but the grease worked into a hemp strop to make it slip round the mast prevents it from breaking when bent (Fig. IVA).

This does not help us to hoist the yard of a lug or sliding gunter close up, but a swivelling masthead sheave might be designed on the lines of a furniture castor, the spindle on which it turns being hollow and forming a lead for the halyard.

This is easy, and has in fact been done, where the mast is hollow and the halyard runs up inside it; not so easy with a solid mast, when the spindle on which the fitting pivots has to be offset and more or less inclined. I suggest in Fig. IXD a rather costly and complicated gadget, though it is hardly worth while unless the height of the mast is absolutely limited; remember that if you have a valid excuse for lengthening the mast you get a bigger jib.

I have said that the boom should be rolled up by means of jaws, but any boom, roller or no, should have jaws, which rotate round the mast, rather than a gooseneck fixed to the mast and straining the tack of the sail whenever the boom is squared off, just as the fixed masthead sheave strains the halyard when the yard is squared. But the gooseneck is correct, and nothing I can say will prevent its use. Only let us not use the yacht pattern, which strains and wears out itself and the mast, but the fisherman's, which is mechanically sound and far cheaper. It is simply a hook on the end of the boom engaging in an eye on the mast, so that the thrust comes on the centre of the mastband, not an inch or more above it (Fig. XE). Don't omit the band and just stick a spiked eye into the mast; it need not be a complete band, a plate going a third of the way round the mast and fixed with two screws will do. As the hook is a loose fit in the eye, this gooseneck will not go with roller reefing. The more elaborate pattern figured on the same drawing is sound (Fig. XF).

Many of the gooseneck bands one sees bristle with belaying pins. Cut off any there may be on the fore side of the mast, or they will certainly make trouble with the jib sheets. The pins are sure to be inconveniently small anyway, and you can put better ones in the thwart, where they will not foul anything.

Wooden gaff jaws are a mistake, as are any sort of jaws which have to be held in to the mast by a rope or wire parrel line, because the points of the jaws are apt to pick up halyards and other ropes as they slue round the mast. Now the beauty of the gaff rig for a boat, as opposed to a larger yacht, is that you can bring the main halyards down on the fore side of the mast, where the gaff itself cannot touch them, if they can be prevented from being chewed up by the jaws. No one ever detaches a gaff from the mast except when laying up at the end of the season, and if he did want to do so it is easier to detach the gaff from iron jaws than to detach the jaws from the mast, so I use a complete iron band, which cannot pick up things, instead. The material of mine is light enough to spring it on and off the mast without permanently distorting it, but that would not be necessary on a boat's mast which can be unstepped without the use of a crane. The whole fitting is lighter and stronger, as well as safer, than the iron jaws you buy (Fig. XD). Note that if a lower throat halyard block is used either the lugs on the mastband must be extended or the side-straps on the gaff angled, so that if the throat halyards were accidentally let go or from any other cause the gaff were left hanging from the peak it would not be broken against the block. If using the Norfolk rig do not make the single halyard fast at the extreme peak, or the gaff is liable to up-end in a gybe.

The iron mast traveller or parrel used to hold in a lug yard is generally of un-suitable design. It is a hoop with an eye standing up from it and a hook hanging down; the halyard is spliced to the eye and the yard hung on the hook. This is not seriously troublesome if the sail has a short yard and a long luff, but dinghies' lugs are rather the other way, and, when they have a reef in, the luff is pretty sure to be shorter than the yard between the heel and the slings, where it is hooked to the traveller. In such a case the yard will not come right down unless the tack is let go. A much handier form of traveller has a fixed eye extending horizontally from the hoop—a good brass thimble seized on with wire makes the best job—and the halyard is rove through the eye and bent to the yard with no hooks (Fig. IIIA). Now, when you lower, the halyard renders through the eye and you can pull the yard away from the mast and stow it as you like, with no need for going forward to unhook it. But I might mention that when close-hauled and well reefed down the traveller may ride up the mast and allow the yard to be pulled too far aft; there ought perhaps to be a light piece of line attached to the traveller to hold it down. In a small boat, however, we can get along very well with no traveller at all. It is not wanted when the yard is hoisted up, and when reefing it is a moment's work to rig a running parrel of rope.

There is no need to keep a strop on the yard to bend the halyard to; hitch it straight round the spar or splice an eye in the end, if it can be slipped on over the end of the spar, and then there are no obstructions to prevent the sail being slid off for dry storage, except a little wood cleat screwed on under the yard to keep the hitch from slipping up it. Before hoisting see that the hitch is pulled up tight and that the halyard comes exactly opposite the cleat; if it slips round you will be winding the peak of the sail round the yard, which will do it no good. I see no reason why the peak halyard should have more points of attachment to a boat's gaff than the single halyard to the longer lug-yard, so bend it on in the same way and you can slide the sail off the gaff just as easily. It is traditional to use a stunsail halyard bend, shown in Fig. XIIIK, because it brings the yard up snugly to the sheave, and also, if properly made, doesn't slip; but don't omit the cleat on the strength of that, because it shows you where to put the bend, also, if the spar is well greased for the sake of the stops on the head of the sail, the bend will slip up it.

The really economical man splices a couple of feet of chain to the end of a lug or sliding gunter halyard, where it is liable to chafe in the masthead sheave-hole and the parrel. To make a chain splice, unlay about 9 inches of the rope, and pass two strands through the end link of the chain; unlay the third strand, and lay up one of the others in the groove it leaves, and join them as in a long splice, with an overhand knot and two tucks against the lay of the rope. In making the overhand knot the strands go round each other the same way that the yarns go round them. The ends of the strands in a long splice which is constantly being bent round a sheave, as here, are apt to come untucked, so marl them down with palm and needle to the strand they are tucked under, not round the whole rope. You have now a good three-strand rope as far as the link, and two strands through it, but one of them has nowhere to go. Tuck it into the rope, backing it round with three tucks against the lay. It will not look very tidy at first, but will soon pull out smooth and render easily over the sheave. Two strands of 1½-inch rope will go through a link of $^3/_{16}$-inch long-link chain, and that will go through a ⅝-inch sheave-hole, which is the narrowest you would use for that rope, anyway. Do not shackle the end of the chain to a strop on a lug yard; pass it round the yard and secure with a large shackle to its own part, so as to make a running noose of it. If the wood of the spar is very soft sew a bit of leather or canvas round it.

I am supposing that three-strand rope is used, as it should be. Four-strand stuff is sometimes seen in boat's gear, but it has no virtues and many faults in small sizes. It is weaker than three-strand; it pulls down more, the strands losing their lay in one place and running into kinks elsewhere; it makes a clumsier splice. An eye-splice round a block or thimble with Manilla rope has to be made very snug and pulled up very tight, or it will stretch so much that the block drops out. I use an unorthodox but effective method of making it snug. Enter two strands between the same pair of strands on the standing part, bringing one out under the left-hand strand and one under the right-hand, and heave them up as tight as you can round the block. Miss the first tuck with the third strand, but begin the second tuck by putting it under the second strand to the left, and carry on round with the other strands as in a normal splice; one more tuck all round finishes it. Most yacht riggers serve over splices, to hide the ends of the yarns, which stick out if they are left long and draw out if they are cut short; the serving is apt to work loose as the splice stretches and pulls down, and I don't think it's really an improvement. I don't taper the strands, but let them stick out half an inch, and I don't think anyone ever notices them.

The strands of a wire splice on the other hand must be tapered carefully. The wire does not break in the splice itself, but just above it, where it has been some-what weakened by opening out the strands, and where its diameter is reduced; so that reduction must be made as gradually as possible. If it is not, e.g. if the last tuck has been made with whole strands, not only have the strands of the stand-ing part been opened out more than necessary but they lead from the splice to the untouched part at an unnatural angle, and that is where they break.[1] There is a proverb, 'As many ships so many wire splices', so I will give no instructions about making them, except to say that we have no use for one made 'under and over', tucked against the lay of the rope, like a rope splice. It is easier, neater, and just as strong to wind each strand round and round the first one you tuck it under, following the twist of the wires. A splice so made with iron wire is so smooth as to be almost invisible; but do not on the strength of that leave it uncovered. The ends of wires which may be almost invisible may tear your hands badly and your marling-spike will have knocked some of the zinc coating off them and exposed them to rust. Cover the splice, and a good inch above it, with calico soaked in tar or white lead or with insulating tape and serve over with stout sail twine. Serving is often done with a thin hard stuff called 'yacht marline', but that ought not to be used for any purpose except fancy work. The essence of a serving or a seizing

---

1   I understand that splices in stainless steel wire are not to be trusted. This looks as though the material becomes brittle when roughly handled; if so it should be avoided altogether.

is that the turns should be packed into a solid mass which is almost imperishable and, in the case of a serving, quite watertight. Only soft cordage will pack like that; yacht marline, lacking the continuous contact, is liable to work loose. Even if it is drowned in varnish, that may crack and let the water into a serving, and if there is any play in a seizing the parts will chafe and soon break. If you cannot get tarred roping twine or good small tarred spunyarn try this way of making a serving with untarred stuff. Soak your parcelling—a strip of calico wound spirally round the wire—in Stockholm tar before you put it on; it will stick without any need to marl it down. Now put on the serving as tight as you can—you can't break the stuff—and if you are not using a serving board rub it down as you go with your finger or a bit of wood; the tar will be squeezed into the twine and impregnate it thoroughly. It is a messy job, but the result is neat and everlasting.

When things get adrift it is usually because a clip-hook has shaken loose, a pin dropped out of a shackle, or a rope slipped off a cleat to which it was belayed. The clip-hook is easily dealt with. Put an indiarubber ring, as tight as you can get it on, round the necks of the hooks, and you can't lose or forget it, as you might a mousing. Where possible use clip-hooks rather than shackles; I have twice lost sails through shackles breaking; never from a clip-hook. The pins of shackles come unscrewed unless they are wired in, and it is too easy to drop the pin or the shackle itself overboard.

All the shackles used in boats have pins that screw in with an eye in the end to turn them with the point of a marling-spike; the eye is often so small that the point of the spike won't enter, or breaks off if the screw is a bit tight; one ought to carry a small footprint spanner in one's pocket rather than a marling-spike. For a shackle which has to be shifted often, it might be worth while to adopt a pattern (Fig. IXʙ) in which the pin is not screwed but has a key-end which passes through a key-way and is locked by a half-turn, the key being held in that position by being drawn into a shallow slot by a spring. But small springs are perishable and not easy to replace, so I prefer to hold the key in its slot by screwing down a wing-nut against the eye of the shackle; the nut can be screwed tight enough with the finger and thumb, and a turn and a half or two turns back give the key enough clearance to allow the pin to rotate. As the key-way is cut only half-way through the eye next the nut, the key cannot pass through it and allow the pin to drop out.

Unless it is prevented from turning, the bolt connecting the gaff to iron jaws is apt to drop out. It may have a short key under its head, to engage in a key-way cut in the nearer side-plate, but that is unlikely. The further side-plate may be threaded for it to screw into; if the thread on the bolt projects far enough through the plate to get a lock-nut on, this is neat and effective. If both holes are plain, nothing will stop the bolt from turning, but you must keep the nut on it by putting a lock-nut over it, or by using a turret-head nut, which has slots cut in it so that a pin through the bolt engages in them and keeps it from turning.

Most small metal cleats of stock pattern are badly designed. Their base is too short to give wood screws a chance of holding it firmly; their arms are too thin and join the base with an angle instead of an easy curve that a rope will render over; and their points stick out needlessly far, and if there's nothing else for them to foul they tear your clothes. A long flat wooden cleat, even if it projects a quarter of an inch more, is far less obstructive and dangerous, and the score for the rope can be made nicely rounded. You can't haul in a jib sheet by hand and then take it round a tiny cleat with any certainty that you have got it the right tautness; get it on a decent big cleat first and then you can slip it round whichever way is wanted to trim the sail exactly, with no risk of barking your knuckles. A good wooden cleat might have actually less projection than an iron one, because you don't have to make a dash for it while you are hanging on to the rope. Jamming cleats are particularly nasty, and I can see no reason for them at all; if you want to jam a rope it's better tucked under its own part (Fig. XG). Anyway, the arms of the cleat ought to be long enough to take two turns of the rope comfortably, in case you want to belay it properly. Unless you are using an outsize jib you never want to let the sheet go in a desperate hurry. A jib slatting with its sheets flying prevents the boat from luffing more than if it were trimmed fairly easy, as it should be in squally weather.

The first law of boat-sailing is that the main sheet must never be belayed but must be held in the hand. But that does not forbid its being held round a cleat or pin, if there is no possibility of its jamming. I would rather ease the strain on my hand that way by multiplying blocks on the sheet and lengthening the rope. Simple gear and short ropes spell safety.

XI

SAILS AND FANCY RIGS

A BOAT'S SAIL SHOULD BE LIGHT, to be of use in fine weather, and it
may still be amply strong for heavy weather, if it gets fair treatment. Small
sails are almost always cotton—sixteen years ago I had some of aeroplane linen,
but I don't know if that is procurable now—and cotton is very readily attacked
by mildew. Unless they can be covered with a really waterproof coat, and unless
they are really dry when coated, they should be taken ashore. (But if they have to
stay aboard wet, see that they are wet with salt water, not with rain.) So the careful boat-owner, in choosing a rig, will consider the facility it gives for unbending
and transporting his sails. If, as would appear, these are impossible in the case
of a roller jib, the thing stands sufficiently condemned. The mainsail is a more
precious thing, and deserves better care. Some kinds can be unbent in less than a
minute, and therefore have a better chance of being taken ashore than those more
permanently attached to their spars.

My method of bending a sail to a gaff or a lug yard is not only the quickest way
of getting it on and off but it is the only way that gives the sail fair treatment.

Sailcloth shrinks about one foot in twenty when it gets wet. We ease up the
halyard of a lugsail for a shower, or the sail girts till it looks like nothing on earth;
we may ease up the peak halyards of a gaff sail for the same reason; we may even
slack away the clew outhaul of a boom sail if we remember that otherwise its foot
will be strained. But the head of the sail is out of reach and therefore out of mind.
The text-book precept for bending a sail is this: make fast the nock to the jaws of
the gaff or heel of the yard and haul out the peak to the correct tautness. (Who is
to say what is the correct tautness, unless there is a hygrometer aboard?) Then
pull the head of the sail up to the spar with marling hitches at every hole with
a continuous lacing—probably of hambro line, which is the worst material for
shrinking I know. You bend the sail on a fine day, but sooner or later it gets caught
out in the rain. Your original estimate of length may be right, but that lacing may
have shifted, gripping the sail so that it is not evenly stretched between its ends.
I do not call that fair treatment. This is what I do instead (Fig. XIA). Make fast

101

the peak earing—this is a loop of strong line spliced through the cringle, rove upwards through a large hole in the end of the spar, and the bight pushed over the end—an almost instantaneous operation; bend the head of the sail with separate stops of a single part of good line, so loose that however wet they are they will slide easily up and down the spar—if, like the lug yard, there are no permanent fittings on it they slide right off the end, without unknotting from the sail, another almost instantaneous operation—that at the nock, where there is a big cringle to accommodate it, being a stout hemp grommet, but no tighter than the rest, and kept greased, like all of them. Now, when the gaff or yard is peaked and the tack bowsed down, part of the pull on the stout luff-rope will be passed on, by the slipping down the spar of the nock grommet, to the more lightly roped head of the sail all the way up to the peak. The strains are even all over the sail, and if it wants to shrink, you have only to slack up the tack and the head is eased as much as the luff. And that may not be yachting, but it is logic. The tight lacing may look neater, but the distorted seams at the head of a badly-stretched mainsail are more conspicuous than the most untidy stops. They need not look untidy. Make them of stuff so thick that you can just get two parts of it through the hole in the head of the sail, and cross them through the hole. If you can slide them off a naked yard, knot them at the hole; a neat and almost invisible way is to make an overhand knot with each end round the other part, as a fisherman ties a cast; but if they have to be untied the knot is better made over the top of the spar. If the holes in the sail are so small that you cannot get more than one part of a decent-sized stop through them it must be tightly knotted or seized with sail-twine across the headrope, for if the eyelet in the hole is allowed to shift on it, it will be cut very soon; lacings always part here, for that reason. The stop will not be cut by shifting on the greased spar (Fig. XIA).

The critic will say that when the sail is new or wet its nock will come a foot away from the gaff jaws. Why not, if he uses a lacing instead of mast-hoops, as I should recommend in any case? The only use I have for mast-hoops is as a ladder to go aloft, and one doesn't go aloft in a boat. You cannot prevent a certain amount of chafe on a mast lacing, but if it's rove the right way the chafe is not more serious than the chance of a mast-hoop seizing parting. To lace a sail to the mast (Fig. XIA): seize a small brass thimble to each hole in the luff at right-angles to the luff-rope with figure-of-eight turns of spunyarn hove well taut and round turns over them between thimble and roping to make the job rigid; splice the lacing to the nock cringle or to a hoop on the mast; take it round the mast and down through the top thimble, then back round the mast the way it came and through the second, back again for the third, and so on. A lacing rove in this way never jams. And if the sail is 6 or 8 inches away from the mast it draws all the better for that. One more virtue of a lacing, this in connexion with roller reefing. When reefed down to the limit it commonly happens that the boom end drops dangerously, and this is just the time when you want it as high as possible, to clear wave-crests. Increase the diameter of the after-end of the boom, and you do raise it as you roll, but you wind up the sail away from the mast. With the lacing to slack this doesn't matter; the sail cocks up at a queer angle, but it keeps its original shape with no unfair strains on it.

There is no good reason for lacing a boat's sail to a boom, except for roller reefing; true, both the boom and the foot of a loose-footed sail must be stronger, but the extra weight involved is compensated by the sail being more effective, less pressing to the boat, and easier to handle. If a lacing is used it goes round the boom spirally; never let it pin the foot of the sail down tight to the spar, and to make the most of light winds ease it up well.

Nothing elaborate is wanted in the way of reefing gear. Unless you have roller gear, enabling you to reef with the boom over the side, you must get it right amidships to tie the points, for you can't have a man's weight down to leeward, and with it amidships you can pull down the leach cringle to it with a simple lashing, so there is no need to have long reef pendants rove off; generally it would be less trouble and safer to have the whole sail down and hoist it again when the reef is tied in. With a second man in the boat she can be kept sailing easy while the reefing is in progress, but I doubt whether it is wise for a single-hander to try to reef and steer at the same time, even with roller gear. There are two forms of this which might allow him to do so; the so-called Jersey patent, and the worm gear. The first consists of a wire wound round a drum on the boom, led aft through a block at the foot of the mast, and hauled down with a tackle; this is much the better form, because the wire, serving as tack tackle as well as reefing gear, takes all the twisting strain of the boom off the gooseneck or jaws. The worm gear, actuated by a light endless chain passing over a sprocket wheel, leaves the strain on the gooseneck, and would not be worth the expense, which would be considerable, for it is not a stock article. In a gaff sail which is boomless or not fitted with roller gear a balance reef can be taken quickly, if untidily, as described for the lugsail on p. 43.

However light it is a sail is not likely to be blown out of a boat while it is full and drawing; she would capsize first. But it must be remembered that the strength of a sail is proportioned not to its size but to the weight and stiffness of the boat, and in a fresh breeze a heavy boat under very short canvas wants that canvas good and strong, especially as it may not be possible to keep the sail from shaking occasionally, which is what does the harm to it. If the sail is strong enough to stand in blowing weather, however, it will be too heavy for efficiency in light weather. The advantage of being able to change a large light lug for a small heavy one is obvious; it is just as easy to change the Bermudan, and better, because a deep reef in that shifts the position of the centre of effort so far forward that the boat may become unmanageable. So make the smaller sail or trysail the whole length of the boom but only half that of the mast. It is rather more trouble to shift a gaff, and I have never seen a gaff trysail on anything smaller than a ten-ton yacht, so we may leave that out of the question for boats; but no one, as far as I know, has ever tried a simple form of topsail over a small gaff mainsail, which seems very suitable for boats (Fig. XIB). I said it was probably easiest to lower the mainsail right down to reef it; let us try lowering it right down to set a topsail over it. The topsail is bent to a yard the whole length of its luff, and the heel of the yard hooked to an eye on one side of the gaff jaws, and a rope becket on the clew of the sail slipped over the peak of the gaff. The yard can hang from this while the mainsail is being hoisted, then it is straightened up by the halyard, which is the only extra rope aloft. Lowering would be easy if the topsail were to leeward of the peak halyards, for it would fall down into the lee of the mainsail; not quite so easy if to windward, and it might be desirable to have a line bent to the yard to haul it down on its proper side of the gaff. This rig has the merit that the lightest part of it is on top, and the biggest topsail can be very large and light indeed.

I have tried a rig the same shape as the gaff-topsail, but with the sail all in one piece, and reefing on the foot, so the upper part of it and its yard had to be heavier than the detachable topsail. But in light weather the gunter-sprit, as I call it, makes up for the extra weight aloft by its greater flexibility, for the lower gunter-iron exerts much less thrust on the mast than gaff jaws do, and the faintest air swings the sprit and keeps the sail drawing. The rig has the ordinary sliding-gunter fittings, but there is a sprit—it would be a wishbone nowadays—attached to the lower iron by a strong pivot which allows it to move up and down but must not allow the least sideways movement (Fig. XIc). In my thirteen-foot boat so rigged the weight of the sprit and the pull on the leach of the sail were taken by the topmast, some 6 feet of which extended without any staying above the upper gunter-iron, and I believe that topmast has survived for twelve years, but if there were any doubt about the safety of this practice it would be easy to fit a fixed wire lift from the upper iron to the sprit. This rig was particularly handy for the work the boat had to do, which included going alongside piers and ships in a strong tideway, because it was easy to reduce sail, still keeping what was left good and drawing, the upper part of the sail remaining stretched between the sprit and topmast till the heel of the latter was right down on the mast-clamp. For a quick furl the sail was brailed up to the mast, but to stow it, the two spars had to be folded down aft into the boat, like the single spar of the ordinary sliding gunter, and the lower iron disconnected from the mast. They were rather a nuisance to stow, but hardly more so than a gaff, and the gear was simpler; a single tye halyard, no other ropes aloft.

In the popular fisherman's 'lug and mizzen' rig the mizzen is a very small affair, no more than a steering sail, and its mast is stepped practically on the transom, a little to one side of the stern-post, so that the tiller, which is shipped on the opposite side of the rudder, can clear it. The sail is of course sheeted to a bumkin or outrigger, a spar projecting aft through the transom. The sail is either a leg-of-mutton or a standing lug. If it is a lug I see no use in giving it a swinging boom; for all practical purposes it sets as well sheeted direct to the end of the outrigger, if this is long enough, and there is no need to cut it short. It has to be rigged in in any case in a crowded harbour, whatever length it is. Then it is easy to clear away the lug sail, or stow it up and down the mast. The leg-of-mutton generally has a shorter outrigger and a separate boom, which is topped up and down the mast by a topping lift to get it out of the way, and the sail furled to the mast, to which it is bent permanently.

So far I have been thinking of the conventional sailing boat, which has considerable beam in proportion to its length, and enough natural stability to sail without ballast. But one may be tempted to buy a longer and narrower boat, a ship's boat, or a Service or coastguard whaler, and she may prove an excellent bargain if she is rigged suitably. Being rather deficient in stability she will not stand up to one large lofty sail, even with ballast, but she will want plenty of canvas to drive her greater weight; it must be kept low, and therefore should be more evenly distributed on two masts, both well inboard. The twentyseven-foot Service whaler is much under-canvassed; my twentyfour-foot whaler carried more sail, and had about a foot less beam, her mizzen was more than half the size of the mainsail, while the Navy use a mizzen less than a third of the same-sized mainsail. I think a twentyfour-foot boat could be given 240 square feet of sail, provided that that could easily be reduced.

In rigging a large pulling boat the position of the masts is to some extent governed by that of the thwarts, though in some Service boats there is a fore and aft plank between the first two or three thwarts with holes in it for alternative mast steps. In any case the masts are supported at the level of the thwarts, not by a beam across the gunwales, so they must be properly stayed, and as they will not be lowered very often they may be of any reasonable length. In a four-oar boat such as my old whaler they will come about 7 feet in from each end, with 10 feet between them. I carried about 200 square feet of sail in two lugs and a jib; I could have done with a bigger mainsail, but not as a lug. The gunter sprit, if I had then known of it, would have been ideal as the mainsail of a ketch with a tall mizzen mast. The wishbone ketch does not seem to be a great success, but it does show the advantage of sheeting the mainsail to the mizzen masthead instead of to the deck. The rig I suggest in Fig. XIc has none of the disadvantages of the wishbone and all its advantages, and the additional one that the mainsail can be reduced instantaneously to half its original area. (Note: With this rig the automatic gunter-iron described on p. 51 and Fig. VIb must not be used, for if lowered too far the spars would come adrift and fall foul of the mizzen mast.)

Since the sprit always makes the same angle with the mast the end of it may come within an inch of the mizzen mast and still never touch it, whatever height it is hoisted to; therefore it completely fills the space between the masts, which a gaff sail cannot do. A rope is made fast to the mizzen masthead, rove through a thimble on the end of the sprit, and belayed at the foot of that mast; the sprit, sliding up or down this mast-rope, is under control all the time; it is in fact the main sheet, for it takes most of the weight off the clew of the sail. I have tried out the principle on my twenty-ton yacht, not indeed with a gunter sprit, which I am only recommending from personal experience as a boat's sail, but with a gaff and topsail of just the same shape; and I found trimming sail absurdly easy. With a single-part mast-rope I could pull the gaff flat amidships when a yachtsman's gale was blowing, and a single whip on the clew was ample for the lower sheet. The peculiar advantage of the gunter sprit is that in reefing you have only the halyards to look after, the rest looks after itself. When the heel of the sprit is right down on the thwart there is only about 6 feet of the leach of the sail loose, as I have drawn it, and less than 30 square feet of sail area; the weakest man could hardly fail to get hold of the close reef cringle and secure it, and I should keep a lazy sheet made fast to that cringle to make it easy to catch.

My yacht's mainsail has no boom, and this raises the problem of sheeting such a sail; should the sheet be inside or outside the mizzen rigging? I chafed through many main sheets before I realized that the sail ought to be sheeted from the peak as well as from the clew. Then, having taken most of the weight off the clew, I sheeted it thus. A rope is made fast to one side of the mizzen rigging at the height of the clew, rove through the clew cringle, then through a bull's-eye at the same height on the other side of the rigging, and belayed. When this is hauled taut it forms a horse on which the mainsail trims itself across in stays with no attention. Admittedly when it is eased for a free reach it does not set the sail so well as a sheet outside the rigging, but if the reach is a long one it is not much trouble to hook on an outside sheet, and all the time the upper sheet is trimming most of the sail perfectly. If in squally weather you leave a bit of slack in the lower sheet and keep a hand on the upper one or mast-rope you can spill the wind out of the sail at will, and even for close-hauled work its set is not much spoiled.

Because the mainsail, being trimmed to the same angle all over, need not be trimmed very flat anywhere, it does not backwind the mizzen as in a common ketch. The mizzen is a worthwhile sail, and, with a fine tall mast to carry it, can be a pretty big one, if it is so rigged that one man can take it in without involving

the helm in its folds; it will not pull the mast out of the boat, because that is supported by the mast-rope from the end of the sprit. The sail would naturally be a
Bermudan, and, as there are no obstructions on the mast, bent with hoops or a
lacing rather than to a track. That means the topping-lift would have to lead to
the masthead, and it would not top the boom up as snugly as if it came lower; but
the boom would be rather long for that treatment, anyway. I should prefer not to
lace the sail to it, but to put the clew on a traveller running the whole length of it.
When stowing a mizzen is urgent the boat is generally running before the wind;
then by letting go the outhaul the sail would almost stow itself. Now set up the lift
and the mizzen sheet good and hard; the main sprit is putting a great forward drag
on the masthead, and it has no other backstays.

In spite of its forward position the mainsail, with its controlled sprit, is not a
pressing sail, and one could carry the whole of it running before a fresh breeze. I
have been more generous with an area of 150 square feet, against the 120 of my
own whaler's lug mainsail, because this one can be reduced certainly and instantaneously to half its size on any point of sailing.

The mizzen sheet cannot be held in the helmsman's hand, but must be belayed somewhere accessible and clear of the tiller. In a transom-sterned boat one
end may be made fast on one quarter, and the sheet rove through a block on the
boom and a lead-block on the other quarter, to belay on the gunwale. In a sharp-
sterned boat this brings the sheet, and the pull on the boom, very far inboard; it
is better to fix on the stern-post an iron hoop enclosing the tiller, and shackle the
end of the sheet to that, leading it forward through a block on the boom to belay
on the mast. Or a bumkin may be fitted on one quarter, angled so that its end is on
the centre line abaft the rudder, and the boom sheeted to that. Fishermen sheet
quite big mizzens to fixed outriggers, but these are gaff or lug sails, short on the
head and long on the foot, and the outrigger has to be of inordinate length to sheet
them properly; it would not sheet a Bermuda sail at all well, anyway.

It is the fashion in racing craft to put the jib tack only a very short way forward
of the mast, so that half or more of the sail overlaps the mainsail. This is all right
for those who keep a man standing in a cage forward of all, to haul the jib round
the mast when tacking, but all wrong for us, who have to trim it across by the
sheets only, and find those a handful. In the old-fashioned cutter the working jib

was made so that the clew of it cleared, or almost cleared, the forestay; when tacking you left the sheet fast, or at the most eased it a few inches; when the ship was well round on the new tack you took in the slack of what was now the lee sheet and belayed it for a full due, let go the other at your leisure, and the sail was correctly trimmed without any pulley-hauley or slatting of canvas. If for forestay we read mast, and put our jib-sheet leads well aft, we can do in a boat just as easily what is usually the most troublesome of operations and is most often and most conspicuously bungled. If it is an inviolable rule that the main sheet must always be kept in the hand, a man sailing alone must never let the jib sheet get adrift, for he hasn't a spare hand to grab for it.

Another way of keeping it under control is to make it fast to a ring running on a horse, a rope stretched across the boat from gunwale to gunwale just forward of the mast, as is common practice with the fore-staysail sheets of larger craft; if the sail is cut rather low at the clew it will trim itself across in stays with no attention at all. For our purposes one end of the horse should pass through a block or bull's-eye on the gunwale and be belayed within the helmsman's reach, so that he can slack it up to ease the sheet.

To understand why one sail suits a particular type of boat more than another we must know something about the dynamics of sailing. The pressure of a beam wind on a sail trimmed at an angle to it is resolved into two components, one pushing the boat ahead and the other pushing her sideways. Since the resistance of the water to the forward movement of the hull is the lesser the boat makes more headway than leeway, though the force acting to leeward may be the greater. By trimming the sail more fore and aft a greater surface is exposed to the wind pressure, but this makes no difference to the forward force, for the increased pressure is less effectively used, whereas the force acting to leeward increases rapidly. The best angle therefore depends on the ratio between the head resistance of the vessel and her resistance to leeway and to heeling. A shallow boat, or one with little stability, must have her sails trimmed at a small angle to the wind. One easily driven ahead through the water but offering great lateral resistance can trim her sails flatter and up to a point increase her speed, as a car goes faster in high gear, by doing so; but her power to overcome head resistance falls off proportionately. As one alters course and brings the wind more on the bow the forward component of its pressure on the sail decreases in proportion to the sideways pressure, till there is not enough left to overcome head resistance; a hull that is hard to drive soon reaches this point, and no alteration to her sails, the total area remaining the same, will postpone it. But a hull which can be driven by a very small fraction of the wind force can profitably be rigged with sails which give effect to that force when it is applied to them at an extremely small angle. Racing sails are so made, because races are won by windward work, though they may not be the best type on all points of sailing.

The trimming of sails could be expressed by a mathematical formula if they were plane surfaces and if the friction and the resistance of the wind could be neglected and if the hull resistance increased regularly with the speed; but none of these things are so. Square sails, and racing mainsails sheeted as hard as they can be got, have their head and foot approximately in the same plane, but they have more or less of a belly in the middle; aeroplane designers have proved, what we have long known, that a suitably curved surface has more lift than a flat one. But square sails are not practical for our purpose; we do not always want to sheet a fore-and-aft mainsail as hard as we can, and if we did so in most boats they would not sail at all. Wind resistance becomes serious when we are sailing very close-hauled; to reduce it spars and rigging are cut down to, and sometimes below, the limit of safety, and friction is reduced by making sails with the seams running in the same direction as the air-flow; not a good practice on the score of strength and durability, but, perhaps because it is easier for the sailmaker, indiscriminately adopted. The problems of hull resistance concern heavy ballasted yachts more than boats, but every vessel has an economical speed, to exceed which a large increase of power is wanted. When working to windward it is uneconomical to fall below this speed for the sake of lying half a point closer to the wind, since the faster a boat travels the less leeway she makes. For a boat which could not sail profitably four points off the wind, and for any boat when such a course is not wanted, the sails should be really effective at five or six points off the wind; that is, as much as possible of their area must present the correct angle to the wind and take the right curvature when the sheet is eased. Here the tall narrow sail breaks down, for its upper part contributes no propulsive force, and in fact adds to the windage of the mast needed to support it, while the foot of the sail is still sheeted too flat for good results.

The pulling effect of the luff (so successfully exploited by the tall racing sail) is due to the fact that a partial vacuum is formed on the lee side of it, and if the canvas has the right amount of slack it is drawn into the vacuum in a curve which bulges against the wind in a manner otherwise impossible; this bulge therefore pulls the boat more to windward than pressure on a flat sail could push her. It is most effective when the wind strikes it free from eddies and can pass along its lee side without any obstruction; a jib or staysail therefore pulls better than a mainsail attached to a mast, to leeward of which eddies must be formed. From this point of view the worst attachment is that to a track fixed to the after side of the mast, for it leaves a large pocket to leeward of it to make the eddies. Failing a revolving mast, which is impracticable, the sail is best attached by hoops or a lacing, or bent to a gunter yard, so as to lie always to leeward of the mast. To fill the pockets and produce a stream-line effect a canvas sleeve could be laced to the luff on both sides round the mast, as was done on the 23-metre Shamrock; in a small boat it could be worked with a zip fastener, and there would be no rigging in the way of it, for the mast could be made stout enough to stand without stays. But this is an elaboration which hardly concerns a non-racing boat. A simpler way of improving the set of a gaff sail when close-hauled, if you can spare the space, is to keep its luff a foot or so away from the mast; this is the practice in some Dutch types. But unless one wants to go in for very fine windward work the best sail is that which will at all angles of trim have its head and foot most nearly in the same plane and show a fair curve in its belly.

XII

THE BOAT UNDER OARS

THE GALLEY SLAVE WAS CHAINED TO HIS OAR, not to his paddle or to his yuloh. This does not prove that the oar is the most efficient way of applying man-power to propulsion—it is possible that the state barge of Indo-China, propelled by fifty-eight sculling paddles, would give the galley a good race over a straight course—but the power of manoeuvring was essential to the galley, as it generally is to us when we get into a boat. If I had to abandon a wreck in bad weather I should feel more certain of getting away in a boat with only half a crew of oarsmen than in one driven by any sort of mechanical device. Since so much of our boatwork consists of landing or embarking or coming alongside another vessel I think an outboard motor no substitute for a pair of oars as the alternative to the sails.

The technique of rowing is very simple; it is hardly even a matter of common sense, for it seems to me instinctive to do it in the right way, apart from the nicer points of style. The many people I have seen doing it all wrong must have some queer theory in their minds. At the risk of insulting the reader's intelligence I must instance a case which is not unique. The offender had apparently observed that whenever he could see the blade of an oar it was held at a considerable angle from the vertical, and tried to hold it at the same angle when he was pulling it in the water; he couldn't understand why it went so deep that he could not get it out again at the end of his stroke. That I believe is an unnatural action, anyway. Even if feathering an oar, that is laying the blade more or less flat, were not desirable in order to reduce windage and to avoid striking the tops of waves it would be done involuntarily. You hold the oar with the blade upright when you are pulling on it with your arms straight from the shoulder and your hands in line with them; when you bend your arms at the end of the stroke and lower your hands to bring the oar out of the water you naturally drop your wrists and so turn the oar-blade out of the vertical, and as you swing forward your hands remain in the position for pushing, which is different from that for pulling. It is perverse to try to hold them any other way. So all the rules of style are natural and not arbitrary ones. You do not pull with your arms, because they would soon tire, but with the weight of your body, which will go on for ever; you bend from the hips, because that is where you have the most flexible joint; you keep your back straight, so as to throw the weight of your head and shoulders on the oar. To make certain that your blade has a good hold in the water before you throw your weight on it you drop it in smartly and vertically, or you may find yourself on your back on the bottom of the boat. To recover your balance at the end of the stroke you bring your hands well in to your chest, where you can push them down and so get the blade quickly out of the water, for if you do not make a clean finish the handle of the oar strikes you in the chest and you have 'caught a crab'. And it is obvious that the longer the stroke is kept the fewer separate movements, each an expenditure of energy, are needed in a given distance. It is not hard to acquire the rudiments of oarsmanship, given good conditions—smooth water, a light boat, and well-balanced oars—and it is worth while getting them right then. Faults are unavoidable in bad conditions, but don't let them become habits; least of all proclaim them as virtues, like certain hard-case sea-boatmen, who profess to despise oarsmanship learned on rivers. The long stroke which is so effective in smooth water is of course impossible in a seaway; you can't lie back with your weight on the oar for the boat's pitching may throw your body back beyond its power of recovery, and as you can't be sure of the timing of your finish you must make it too early rather than too late; the beginning must be struck firmly and the oar go deeply in the water. On the forward swing the blades must be raised high enough to clear the waves; do this with your hands only, not by bending your shoulders over the looms, as one sometimes sees done, with the result that when the stroke should be beginning the blades are right up in the air and half the stroke is wasted before they hit the water.

It is difficult to describe the movements of the rower in varying circumstances; it is easier to find out experimentally what sort of stroke best suits the boat and the conditions of wind and sea, with careful regard to these precepts: sit square and keep your eyes in the boat, swing the body from the hips straight fore and aft, keep the back and arms straight, and, as far as possible, maintain a regular rhythm. A heavy boat, or one pulled against a strong wind, makes little progress at each stroke, and however short in distance the rower's swing may be, it is, if the blade of his oars acts as the fulcrum of a lever, long in time; and a stroke which is too slow is as tiring as one which is too quick. The blades of sea oars are therefore made narrow, so that they can be pulled through the water; the slip relieves the rower as propeller slip relieves an overloaded motor. Actually the pivotal point is about where the oar enters the water, or perhaps still nearer to the rowlock; but, even so, that distance is once and a half or twice that from the rowlock to the handle, so it is a lever that does not favour the oarsman much. He naturally wants to get as much of the oar as he can inboard: if he is pulling a single oar, by sitting as far away from the rowlock as possible; if a pair of paddles, by holding them so that the handles just meet when they are raised to depress the blades during the stroke, which means that they will overlap very considerably when the blades are raised out of the water. That is no inconvenience; one hand is kept slightly in advance to clear the other. But trouble does arise when pulling a small boat in rough water, for the handle cannot be depressed enough without striking the rower's knees. A shallow beamy dinghy then, though she may be perfectly safe, is not a good sea-boat, for you have to shorten the oars inboard and so cannot take advantage of her beam to make them more efficient levers. She should have a good depth amidships, even at the cost of more weight and windage.

So much feathering of the blade as is done unconsciously is enough to make it glance clear of a wave-crest if it strikes one, but not enough to nullify the effect of a head wind on it. Indeed half feathering may be worse than no feathering at all, if the blade, making an angle with the wind, soars up like a kite and lifts the oar out of the rowlock. A square river oar naturally lies flat in its square rowlock, but there is nothing to stop a round oar at the right point. It is even worse to turn it too far, for the blade may be forced down into the water. It is curious that square oars, which relieve the wrists of a great and continuous strain, are not generally used at sea. Where they are used they are so fitted that they cannot be feathered, and the blades are made very narrow.

Oars, especially ash ones, are liable to warp, and generally an oar will pull better with one side of the blade than the other, or on one side of the boat rather than the other; it is worth while finding out how a set of oars fits best, and marking them. Bow should have the shortest oar, for he usually has the lightest work. When two men are rowing without a coxswain, stroke pulls with an even effort, leaving it to bow to do the steering by pulling the boat's head round or by easing his pull. If there is a strong beam wind the weather oar generally has all the work, and the bow oar is put that side; even so he may not be able to prevent the boat from running up into the wind, in which case he must pull as hard as he can and leave it to stroke to do the steering.

In some countries oars are not pulled, as we use them, but pushed, the rower standing up and facing forward. The method is not so effective as ours, but at times is useful, as for instance when one has to navigate an intricate channel, or to pick up an object floating in rough water, when the extra height of one's eye gives it a wider range. In such a case with two rowers bow sits at his oar and stroke stands up. A short spell in this changed position might prove restful in the course of a long pull in a large deep boat, but not in a shallow one, where the stooping posture needed would be tiring. Finally, some people, in particular the crews of fishing boats and coasters, fancy sculling with one oar over the stern. I cannot believe that this is really efficient, but every boatman ought to practise it, in case he should lose one of a pair of oars. Stand up facing aft, and hold the longest oar available in the sculling notch with its blade horizontal, and with your wrists well under it. As you move your arms from side to side your wrists automatically cant the blade through a small angle, enough to force it downwards and towards the boat's stern. The tension of your arms prevents it from going right under the boat, which therefore begins to move ahead. As she gathers way you increase the cant, as you might increase the pitch of a propeller, so as to keep a steady pressure on the upper and after side of the blade, and so drive the boat ahead. That pressure of course vanishes during the time in which the oar is being turned to reverse the cant at the end of each stroke, and the boat's headway will force the blade up out of the water unless the reversal and the beginning of the new stroke are made very smartly. Except for this moment of reversal the driving force is continuous, not intermittent as in rowing, but only half of it is effective, the other half merely depressing the boat's stern. The wrist action is just as natural and easy with one hand as with two, if the boat is a light one, and gives the sculler more freedom to look round him.

A boat under oars is more under control than any other craft, but only so long as the oars on both sides have clear water to work in. The novice forgets that when he comes within six feet of an obstruction on his broadside one of his oars goes out of business altogether. One often sees him trying to come alongside a landing-place, and stopping his boat dead some little distance away from it, when nothing he can do with his one free oar will bring him any nearer. The only power he has with one oar is that of modifying the effect of headway already on the boat by holding water or backing; if he pulls he only turns her stem into the obstruction. To come alongside, then, you must bring the boat in at such an angle that backing with the outside oar stops her at the right spot. If there is a strong wind or tide against her she must come in as fast as possible, and at a fairly wide angle, so that both oars are effective up to the last moment, and a vigorous and decisive back stroke must be made to turn her. If the rower fails to catch hold of something to make the boat fast to he cannot do anything more at that attempt; he must push off well clear and have another shot at it. After his last stroke with it the inner oar must be immediately laid inside the boat, and, if there is time for it, the rowlock unshipped; the boat herself will take no harm if she comes alongside with a bit of a bump. There is a common idea that oars should be boated with the blades forward, to avoid scooping water over passengers who may be sitting in the stern. That looks all right, if it comes off, but it is safer to make a rule against it, so that the operation can't be tried when conditions make it difficult or even dangerous. To bring the blade forward, unless you toss it vertically, you are swinging it towards the ship or quay you are approaching, and if you are the least bit late you may strike it and have a bad smash. If on the other hand you lift the oar out of the rowlock by raising the handle, letting the blade trail in the water, you can't hit anything, and you get in at least one more stroke before it becomes unusable.

It is hard to hold on by hand to a vessel anchored in a strong tide, for the boat is apt to sheer out and you may be dragged overboard. Get your painter fast to her as soon as possible. It is not the same thing to catch hold of one of her ropes, because any pull on that, until it is fast to your stem, makes the boat sheer out; and if you are alone in a small boat, shifting your weight forward to make it fast there increases the sheer to a dangerous extent. The same warning applies if a passing motor-boat offers you a tow and throws you a line; don't hang on to it, but bend it to your painter, if you are sure that will run out clear; as a corollary see that the painter is neatly coiled and that the end of it is well amidships, conspicuous and handy. In my boats I have a short hook-rope as well as the painter, and the hook always lies on the thwart I row from; once it is hooked on to anything I can let the boat drop back on it alongside while I boat the oars at my leisure.

Notes: When hooking to a ring always have the point or bill of the hook uppermost or outward. If the hook were on the end of the long painter it wouldn't do, because unless the painter passed through a fairlead on the bow I shouldn't try to haul up by it, having seen boats swamped this way or men dragged out of them.

If you have to tow another, and especially a heavier boat, don't make the rope fast to your transom, or the other will drag your stern all over the place and you will not be able to keep straight ahead of her. Make it fast under the thwart you are rowing from—to the stanchion that supports the thwart, if there is one—and see that the rope can move freely sideways right across your stern, and even broad out on the quarter. If there are obstructions on the transom, lash a spar across it for the rope to slide on. This may not be possible with a whale-boat stern, but if you had a good strong mast you might be able to tow from high enough up that for the rope to clear your head while rowing.

So far I have been considering boat work in fairly smooth water. But every owner of a sea-boat ought to have some idea of what he would do if he had to board a ship at sea, or rescue a man cut off by the tide on a cliff. Boarding a ship which is under way is relatively easy; there are generally plenty of people on deck to help, and she will steer so as to give you a lee. Here, unlike landing alone at a quay, you want to keep your boat away from the side and only bring her close in for an instant; you tow in such a way that she tends to sheer out, and has to be steered in with the rudder or pulled in by a breast-rope. Pass your painter under the bow thwart well before you approach, and bend the heaving-line they throw you to it; when it comes taut it will lead out on the bow and give you the required sheer, and you will tow at a safe distance while they are getting the Jacob's ladder over and you are waiting for a smooth. But when boarding a wreck you haven't this means of keeping the boat clear. She can only be brought in broad-side on with two breast-ropes, fore and aft, while she is kept off by pushing with two spars. With good power at the oars relative to the weight of the boat it would be safer to back her in, the coxswain, if any, unshipping his rudder and standing by with the tiller or a spare stretcher to give a push over the stern which, with a simultaneous stroke of the oars, would take her clear. If the boat has a wide transom with a mizzen mast stepped right aft on it leave the mast standing, to steady a man as he jumps on board. I noticed that the shore boats which ply for hire in Rio harbour and embark their passengers over the stern step a short post here to help them. When bringing a boat in stern first to a wreck it is better not to have any lines between them; if she cannot be kept in position with the oars a fixed line would slue her round broadside on; if she drifts away from the gangway you must pull clear and back her in again. Do not be in a hurry to back her in at an unsuitable moment, and do not wait close in if your man hesitates to jump; your first duty is to your boat, unless you know that others are following you. If you have any doubts about her safety the man must jump into the sea and be hauled into the boat as quickly as possible, before his clothes get thoroughly soaked; wet clothes may be better than no clothes from the point of view of warmth, but they are devilish heavy. A swimmer should always climb into a small boat over the stern. If the man can't swim he must be hauled across on a rope; in that case don't let the boat get too near, in case the men on the wreck don't pay out the rope fast enough and it drags you back.

It is more dangerous to take a castaway off a rock, which is not so straight and smooth as a ship's side, and may be surrounded by shoals and breakers. You may not be able to get near enough for him to jump into the boat, and you probably won't have a long enough line in her to throw to him, so unless he can swim or is in imminent danger it is better not to make the attempt. Back in as far as you safely can, hail him, and tell him you are going for help; and when you get an offing make distress signals on the chance that some passer-by will see them. If you wreck your boat in a place that can't be seen from the top of the cliff you are just as much lost as if you wrecked her out at sea. The recognized distress signal of a ball and a square flag, which may be represented by a cap held at arm's length and a coat hung over the arm, may not catch the attention, being static, and is not generally understood. More people would notice and understand SOS Morsed with a cloth tied to the end of an oar. If a rescue has to be attempted do not be in a hurry. Seas behave in a capricious way; nine running may rise and fall harmlessly on a rock face and the tenth break all over it. A little patience may reveal a place where they never break.

Without a large boat and a strong and skilful crew a ship or a rock can only be approached in very moderate weather, when, once clear away, there is little

danger of the boat's being swamped unless she is overloaded. The chief danger in a small boat is that of a passenger lurching against the gunwale and capsizing her. For this reason when all the oars are manned—double-banked, if possible, and it doesn't matter if the second man on the oar is not an expert; he may not help much, but he is kept out of mischief—the remaining passengers should lie down in the bottom of the boat, where they add to her stability and can bale her, and are out of the way of the rowers. On no account allow anyone to stand up in a boat.

In a heavy sea, even in deep water where there is no tidal stream, enough of the crests breaks to capsize a boat if she gets broadside on to them. She is therefore steered straight at an oncoming sea, with all the speed the oars can give her, so that she cuts through the crest as quickly as possible; the shorter her passage the less water she will ship. If she loses way she may be turned broadside on or even thrown up on end and her stern driven under. If her course is not directly to windward she must make it between the seas; the rowers will have to help the steering, for the rudder does not act quickly enough and a steering oar is hard to manage; you have to stand up to work it, and, even so, at one moment the handle is above your head and the next is foul of your legs. The weights must be kept as much as possible amidships; this makes the boat quicker in turning as well as allowing her to ride over the seas drier.

When rowing to leeward you equally want to shorten the time when the boat is hanging on the crest of the sea; but she is now in a much more dangerous position, for she is already travelling in the same direction as it is. She will be carried forward at something like the speed of the wave, but you cannot let her indulge in this sort of surf-riding. Her bow, which is already depressed, is meeting the resistance of water travelling relatively slowly, and the slightest deviation from a straight course increases that resistance and her stern is thrown round and she is rolled over. In such a case you may have to back at the approach of a sea, or tow astern a bucket or a drogue—a small sea-anchor—to check her way. It is of course absolutely vital to keep her exactly at right angles to the crests as they overtake her. A boat with a large transom is more dangerous than one with a sharp stern; it is often recommended to turn round and back her down wind, the oarsmen being prepared to pull ahead for all they are worth on the approach of a bad breaker, such as one might encounter when crossing a bar or making for a shelving beach.

The worst seas are met where there is a strong tide against the wind, so never try to take a bad bar on the ebb; you can't tell from seaward how bad it is going to be.

If it becomes impossible to handle a boat under oars she will ride safely to a drogue; the longer scope this has the better—the regulation length for a ship's boat's painter is ten fathoms. Your boat will not carry a Board of Trade drogue, and may not even carry a bucket, but you can make a sea-anchor by lashing the bottom boards and spare oars together, and weighting it with the anchor, if you have one. A drogue floating on the surface is carried backwards and forwards by the oscillatory movement of the water, which does not synchronize with that at the distance of the painter's length, so the rope may come slack and allow the boat's head to fall off; the surface drift of the water carries it and the boat to lee-ward very rapidly; so the more immersion it has the better. A proper drogue, which is a canvas cone with its base sewn to an iron hoop, and with a small hole in its apex, has a tripping line bent to the apex so that if you haul on that you are tow-ing it sharp end first and so reduce its resistance; in theory you can regulate your speed by hauling on or slacking away the tripping line, if it hasn't already wound itself round the warp. A weight hung from the hoop of the drogue would prevent that from spinning, especially if the hoop were also buoyed; and if the tripping line were rove through a fairlead on the weight it would be kept clear of the warp (Fig. XII).

XIII

UNDER SAIL

A SAILING BOAT IS ONE OF THE MOST SENSITIVE of man's creations, and the smaller and lighter the more sensitive she is. Therefore I recommend the beginner not to start his sailing in a racing dinghy, but in a craft which is heavy enough to carry her way for some distance if she is allowed to get head to wind, and not so quickly responsive that the rough handling of an inexperienced helmsman sends her flying round in circles. If the novice is going to start alone, in a small boat, one sail is all he needs. A head-sail doesn't really make any difference to her handling, and I think people get into trouble through bungling the jib sheets at least as often as through any other cause. Naturally the boat must be designed to sail without a jib; one which has the mast nearly amidships will be impossible to steer under mainsail only, for she will try to head into the wind like a weathercock. The exact relation between the position of the centre of effort of the sail and the centre of lateral resistance of the boat's hull and centreboard, if any, is not so all-important as is often supposed, and in any case one can't calculate where they will be once the boat begins to move, but there must be some sort of balance between them if she is to steer easily. In a boat with a long keel and no centreboard one can shift the centre of lateral resistance by altering her trim a little, but if she is all centreboard, which can't be shifted, the balance must be attained by the disposition of the sails.

A sail is not entirely useless in a common boat with no centreboard. If it is the right sort of sail and trimmed right she might make good a course of six points off the wind, with a steady breeze in smooth water. To do it the sail must be trimmed so as to make the most of the propulsive force of the wind while escaping as far as possible its sideways force; it must lie at a fine angle to the wind but pretty square across the ship, and the ordinary fore-and-after will not pull its weight like this. A dipping lug, or a gaff or sprit sail with a vang, will; it will keep the boat going hard with her head five points off the wind, and she will not make more than a point of leeway; for, roughly, leeway varies inversely as speed. It is

124

worth remembering, in case your centreboard jams or is lost, that a boat, however rigged, cannot be sailed in the same way without as with it.

A boat with a centreboard or a deep keel can of course be luffed closer to the
wind before her leeway becomes serious, a fact to which she calls attention by sailing conspicuously slower. The point beyond which it does not pay to luff depends
more on the absolute value of the head resistance than on its ratio to the lateral
resistance, because the wind impinging on the sails at a very fine angle has little
propulsive effect. It also depends on the strength of the wind; at low speeds the
resistance of even a slow and heavy boat is negligible, and her large sails keep her
going surprisingly close to the wind; and it depends on the state of the sea, which
stops a beamy boat more than it does a narrow one.

It is commonly assumed that a boat working to windward heads four points
off the actual wind, but that is often flattering her. It may be interesting to note
how near she comes to a right-angle turn when she tacks, but it is fatal to try to
steer compass courses, which may result in as much leeway as headway. A practice which is too common is to sheet the sails as hard as possible and luff till they
threaten to shake, but a well-cut sail so sheeted will stand long after it has ceased
to be any good to the average boat. The only way to lay down rules for steering to
windward is from experiments. If you can get a steady moderate breeze, smooth
water and no tide or current, an accurate compass, and a patent log, plot a series
of tacks on the chart from shore bearings and note what compass courses you
steered and what speed you made through the water; repeating the experiment
with different courses and trim of sails till you find out which is the most profitable combination. You can do it more roughly, without the use of shore bearings
and the log, by timing successive runs between two points, if you are certain that
there is no current.

Let us now imagine an instructional cruise, and put our theoretical knowledge
into practice. I shall assume that our boat is a fair average craft, not a racing type,
rigged with a mainsail and one headsail or jib; and that she is lying on moorings
with clear water all round her. In most boats it takes a certain amount of time
and trouble to set the mainsail, so that is done before dropping the moorings;
the boat will lie quietly head to wind while you are doing it, if there is no tide or
if it is running the same way as the wind. If the tide is against the wind and the

boat starts sailing about as soon as you hoist on the halyards you must let go the mooring, steer clear under jib only, and set the mainsail as and when you can. There should be no difficulty in setting a boat's sail instantly at any time. The superstition that there is derives from the distant days of big racing yachts, when it was really impossible to set their huge jackyard topsails except head to wind, and when those which were Bermuda-rigged had such badly designed slides that they always jammed. If a boat's sail gives trouble there is something quite unnecessarily wrong about it. But let us assume that there is no tide; the boat will lie head to wind with the mainsail set, but not with the jib too—that must not be hoisted till the last moment before the mooring is let go. So stream the mooring buoy on the side which is to be to windward when you get under way, holding on to a bight of the buoy-rope with a single turn, ready to slip; then up jib, with the sheet made fast to windward, and cast off. The boat will take stern way; put the tiller down, but don't let it fly out of your hand, or it will go too far; it will have most effect at about 30 degrees. Ease the main sheet; she will fall off clear to leeward of the buoy till the wind is abeam; then trim jib and mainsail, and she will gather headway at once. This is a safe method for the single-hander, and gives him plenty of time to clear up forward and get aft to the tiller, because the boat will lie quite still till he trims over the jib. If there are obstructions so close to leeward that one cannot afford to take stern-way, some people sail up over their moorings, letting them go when the boat is on the right tack, and so getting away with headway; but this is not very safe. A buoy-rope has a lot of slack, and may have been pulled a considerable distance when let go, and so spring back with some force and perhaps foul the centreboard or rudder; it is essential that it should be seen leading well off the weather bow to make sure that it drops clear. Whether or no there is a navigational reason for casting the ship on one tack rather than the other you must make up your mind which is to be the weather bow, and stick to it; so catch a turn on it with the bight of the buoy-rope and bring the buoy aft outside the rigging, cast off forward and haul on the rope aft, and you will give the boat plenty of headway and at the same time cant her clear of the moorings. It is less trouble to push or pull a boat the way you want her by hand than to mess about with sails and the helm; the proud owner sometimes forgets that his vessel doesn't weigh a ton, so I may inform him that I generally adopt this safe if not so dashing method of getting my yacht, which weighs over 20 tons, away from her moorings. Similarly, if you want to get away from a quay with the wind blowing right on to it, run out a line with a long eye over a bollard well ahead, and haul on it from aft, and you will sheer out far enough to sail clear; make sure before you start that you can flick your line off the bollard, unless there is someone ashore to cast it off—but if there is it is simpler for him to tow you clear. This is far more practical than trying to shove off with oars or boathooks.

Getting away from an anchor is not so easy, because you are never sure just when it will break out; you may trip it before you are right over it, and drag it some distance along the ground, and, anyway, the boat doesn't handle well with the anchor and its rope hanging under her forefoot and the weight of the man lifting it right up in her bow. Try the same principle as when leaving moorings; heave short, and catch a turn forward with a bight of the cable, bringing the rest aft outside the rigging; when the boat cants the right way cast off forward and weigh the anchor over the weather quarter. You will do no harm to her topsides with a light boat anchor. Do not try to get an anchor, or anything else, on board to leeward if there is much wind, or you may capsize.

Now we are under way, but with little or no headway on; we must get the boat under full command at once, especially if there is any tricky navigation to be done or other craft to be avoided, and to do so we must give her plenty of speed. A boat pointing close to the wind and moving slowly will not answer her helm, so ease the main sheet and let her fall off till the wind is broad on her beam, then haul in the sheet gradually as she gathers way, and you can bring her close without losing control. As a matter of fact we have to get in the sheet even if we are continuing on a free reach, because we are trimming our sails not by a weathercock ashore but by our masthead vane, which is affected by our forward motion as well as by the real wind. Our apparent wind may come two points closer on the bow, as is made evident when a fast vessel passes a much slower one; the faster will have her sails trimmed much flatter. A novice in the slower one may think he is being passed because the other has her sheets hauled in, and follow her example, but he will probably do more harm than good; he is exposing more sail to the wind, but exposing it at a less effective angle; there is just enough wind to drive his boat at a certain speed, and he can't make any more of it by altering the trim of the sails.

There is, however, something to be done with the sheet. Even in the open sea the wind does not blow with unchanging force, and in the narrow waters where so much boat-sailing is done it is always puffy. In the lulls you can ease the sheet, because the weight of the boom, or, if there is none, of the gaff or yard, tends to bring the sail inboard, and you want the boom to stay swung well out to spread the maximum of the sail at the correct angle. When the wind increases you have to get in the sheet to keep the head of the sail from falling too far to leeward, unless of course it is trimmed independently by a vang; but do not begin to haul in the sheet before the puff comes. If the wind strikes a sail trimmed too flat across it when the boat is moving slowly it merely heels her over, having little power to accelerate her; even the lightest boat takes an appreciable time to attain her best speed, and it does more harm than good to trim the sail for that speed before she had reached it; and a heavy puff is dangerous to a boat caught with little way on, for she will not answer her helm.

Working to windward one pays more attention to the helm than to the sheet. Puffs vary in direction as well as in force, and we take advantage of the free ones to luff[1] a little closer to our course. But it is fatal for a light boat to be caught too much head-on by a puff, because the windage of her spars will stop her dead before her sails can accelerate her. I make it a rule to bear away and ease the sheet a little on the approach of a puff; I lose nothing by this, because the boat gathers speed quickly and luffs as required as soon as the direction of the wind is determined. Without that speed she would answer the helm badly and might get in irons, that is to say, lose all steerage way. Then she will be out of command till she has fallen off so far that the wind is almost abeam; and if the puff continues fresh, one will have a nasty time getting her sailing again, and may even have to take all the canvas off her. That is why it is unsafe to luff in a squall to ease the boat; ease the sheet, but keep her sailing hard; if she won't stand that, it is time to reef.

Almost any sort of boat will come to stays and pay off on the new tack with steerage way on her in a light wind and smooth water, but even racing dinghies, which in those conditions spin round in an instant, will not do it when much reefed down in a breeze; the windage of their masts takes off all their way in the

---

1   To 'luff' is to steer more to windward.

short moment they are head to wind. When that happens you may be able to get them round by hauling the jib sheet out on the side you want to be to windward, and making a stern-board with reversed helm as described for leaving moorings. This manoeuvre is often necessary with more sluggish craft in bad conditions, and it is perfectly sound and accepted seamanship, though it is never mentioned in amateur sailing books, which recommend you in the circumstances to help her round with an oar—also sound practice, and quicker, if we have the oar shipped ready, but generally we haven't. When making a stern-board the helm must be reversed immediately the boat begins to take stern way, and it must not be put over too hard. If you just let go the tiller it often flies square across the stern, and nothing happens at all; I should like to see rudder and tiller so fitted that they can't move more than 40 degrees either way. I use a very long tiller, and when I let go of it the end drops so that it can't pass out over the gunwale, which stops it at the proper angle; and it can't fly away out of my reach, as it might if it stuck up high enough to clear the gunwale.

To make a tack cleanly and without losing ground you must get all the way you can on the boat before you put the helm down, and put it down gradually to avoid checking her way before she has begun to turn. Beginners often slam the helm hard down at once, which has little effect in turning the boat but a great deal in stopping her. If she will come head to wind with, say, 20 degrees of helm, a smart shove the rest of the way may help her round in case she is sticky. Jib sheets are very often mishandled. A jib flogging about hinders a boat's turning more than if it were left sheeted, but it is a common practice to let everything fly the moment the helm is put down. Leave the sheet fast, or at the most only start it a few inches, till you are head to wind, then trim it over gradually, preventing it as far as possible from flapping. You can only do this if the clew of the jib clears the mast, or comes very little abaft it. Leaving the sheet fast till after a light boat is round on the new tack does little to pay her head off, and stops her way a lot, but with a big modern jib it can't be helped, and while that is being trimmed over it makes a huge bag to hold the head wind and drive the boat astern; such a sail should only be used on long reaches. When the boat is round on the new tack do not be in a hurry to meet her with the helm; let her fall off well, and ease the main sheet; she will have lost a great deal of her speed, however smartly you handle her, and she

must be given a chance to pick that up again before you can trim the sails properly and bring her close on the wind.

Once you start to make a tack in a baffling wind you must stick to it. It is fatal to change your mind if the wind seems to be heading you round. If the new tack sends you back the way you have come it may be only for a moment; if the wind looks like holding that way you can get back on the other tack with very little loss of ground, provided that you are sailing good and hard, but if you try to do it when the boat is not really under command you may lose a great deal more by getting her in irons.

A small boat can sometimes work to windward surprisingly well in a big sea, when she is virtually sailing in smooth water except when actually passing through or over a wave crest. One is often recommended to luff as they approach, to reduce one's speed and so avoid crashing into them too hard. But one wants as much speed as possible to get through them at all; the danger is that a light boat is so easily carried backwards by them. One does luff at the last moment, to take the crests at right angles and so get through them as quickly as one can, and also to avoid being turned broadside on by them, but it is fatal to be left without good steerage way after the crest is passed, for the boat has a tendency to head straight down the back of the wave, and needs a lot of helm to keep her away on her course. A short choppy sea, in which the boat begins to pitch, is much more of a hindrance to her. According to her length and that of the sea there is a certain course and speed, only to be determined by experiment, at which she keeps in step with the waves and sails smoothly through them; it may not look a very profitable course, but on any other she will just bob up and down and get nowhere. This is when weight is wanted, so if you carry breakers or tins for water ballast fill them up, and concentrate them amidships.

A boat may make fair progress to windward in a big sea which is running true with the wind, but in making a passage along the coast, if it has a straight shelving shore, she will get trouble. The wind blows along the coastline, but the seas are deflected by the shallow water and come in on it diagonally, shorter and steeper than in the offing. That means that a vessel sailing close to the wind on the offshore tack would be exactly head to sea, and in fact would not sail at all on that tack. On the other tack she would have the sea abeam, and could sail fast and comfortably, but not for very long, for the heave of the sea would set her inshore rapidly. This is one of the many times when the further one is off-shore the better, so steer straight out, with the wind abeam and the sea nothing less than four points on the bow; carry on steering by the sea, and you will find yourself gradually luffing into the wind, till you can make as good progress on one tack as the other. You may have to go several miles for this, but it pays; keeping close to the shore you would never get anywhere. As novices we have all felt an urge to hug the land, the more familiar element, but we are a great deal safer, as well as more comfortable, in the offing. If it comes on bad out there we have a choice of harbours to run for, just as an airman whose engine stops high up has a choice of landing-grounds; like him, if we get into trouble close to solid earth, it's bad trouble. If we can take things easy and are not worried by thoughts of a lee shore it has to be a bad day when we can't make a square drift one way or the other along the coast, till we have a safe refuge under our lee.

With a fresh breeze off-shore give high land a wide berth. You will have either calms and baffling airs in which you cannot sail, or dangerous squalls, which cannot be predicted from the appearance of the cliffs that generate them. I have seen a boat dismasted a full mile to leeward of a little round island no more than 600 feet high, with no definite ravines or gullies to form wind-funnels down its flanks.

Once we are well to windward of our harbour the run in seems a safe and pleasant prospect; and so it is with the right sort of boat, we can let her go under a press of canvas, making perhaps as much as ten knots. Now if we are running at that speed and feel a nice sailing breeze on our backs it is really a strong wind, enough to reduce us to a mere rag of sail if we were broadside on to it. To run with confidence we want to know, first, that we are not going to let the boat get off her course involuntarily, and second, that, in case we have to alter course for navigational reasons or we are really going too fast for safety, we can get most of the sail off her as she goes. A long boat with her sails well inboard will run safely before almost anything—I do not believe there is any real danger of pooping—but there comes a point when even the best-steering boat runs wild and has to be snugged down, and I have known boats—notably a cat-boat, with a tallish mast right in the eyes of her—which would not steer at all even under a bare pole. I must repeat what I said in the preceding chapter: the danger of running before a sea is that in one phase of it the boat's stern is lifted and carried forward with great velocity by the breaking crest while her bow is depressed in dead water where it meets great resistance; even without sail she may be driven under or pitchpole, or, if she deviates the least from a straight course, the increased pressure on one bow turns her broadside on and she is rolled over. The tall mast of the cat-boat, acting as a lever, helped to depress her bows, and, being a relatively short craft, the longitudinal righting lever was too short to keep her on an even keel, and she had not enough speed for her wedge-shaped bows to lift by planing action. The position of the centre of effort of the sails in relation to that righting lever is all-important. When, by altering my yacht from ketch to schooner, I shifted that centre further aft and lowered it she was not only faster when running but steered better. A boat with flaring bows, the planing action of which lifts them, can carry her sail further forward; if the mast is well raked aft, and the sail is a fairly square-headed lug, which is a truly lifting sail, it may be right in the eyes of her. But with many modern boats and rigs, running before a strong wind is a pastime to be indulged in with great caution.

When there is wind there is sea, and no seas are so true that they do not make a boat running before them yaw about more or less. A boat that is over-canvassed may take a sheer to windward which cannot be checked with the helm, or even with a steering oar; she broaches to, and ships a bad sea or is capsized. Or she may take a sheer the other way, and throw the mainsail across in a gybe. Gybing is the bugbear of the fore-and-aft seaman. With a boomless mainsail, however, even an involuntary gybe with the sheet well out is not likely to lead to serious damage, though the yard or gaff may swing so far forward as to be broken against the lee rigging. In my dinghy, whose mast has no shrouds, I gybe with the sheet slack; the yard rears up on end and the sail blows forward quietly in a bunch—unless it blows over the masthead, as sometimes happens. But a boom goes over with a bang which may dismast a boat or make her broach to, unless the sheet is carefully controlled. It must be got close in before she is brought right before the wind. Now the sail, presenting only its edge to the wind, will have little pressure on it; it will go across from side to side with no fuss—it may do so several times with the boat rolling and yawing in a seaway—but you can't leave it like this for long, or an extra wide yaw will throw her broadside on for all you can do with the helm. You

must get the gybe definitely established, and immediately run the sheet out and
at the same time check with the helm her very strong tendency to broach to; all of
which needs careful timing and smart handling of the tiller and sheet.

Obviously when running before the wind a single-handed man cannot neglect his steering to reef or lower his sail; and the boat, which might keep herself
straight for a few moments with his weight aft, will not be likely to do so if he has
to go forward to get at the halyards. I have been caught like that, luckily in a boat
big enough to be unaffected by the shifting of my weight, and rigged with a heavy
lug yard which fell down all inboard when I cut the halyard. It could of course
have been belayed within reach of the helm, but even so if it were rigged with a
purchase or if the spar were lighter the sail might not come down so promptly. It
would be a good rule to keep a drogue or a bucket bent to a long rope handy, to tow
astern to steady the steering and give one a hand free; or merely towing the rope
may keep her straight enough.

It is unlikely that one would be free to reef the sail while any part of it was set
for running before the wind. It might be done with a balance reef, but few boats
are so rigged that this is possible; generally one would have to get the sail right
down, and let the boat lie to the drogue under jib only while one tied the reef in.
Roller reefing doesn't help, because you have to tend the halyards while you are
rolling up the boom, and that makes it a slow job for a single-hander; and if you
lower the sail right down it is a still slower job to roll it up properly. I prefer the
old way of reefing; but it is apparently not foolproof. I have seen so many sails torn
through the lack of common sense that a warning against the way it happens is
justified. The reef-points or lacing only pass through two thicknesses of canvas,
and are not meant to take any strain; all that should come on the cringles in the
luff and leach, which are secured to three or four thicknesses of canvas and a stout
rope. So do not let anyone touch a reef-point till you are satisfied that both the
cringles are properly lashed down. In a larger vessel there are bee-blocks, long
wooden cleats on either side of the boom, with two or three holes down through
them to which the several leach cringles are hauled down by reef pendants, but
in a small boat these are not wanted, as a plain lashing round the boom is good
enough. There should, however, be marks on the boom to show where the lashings come, then you can start reefing by getting the leach cringle down, and if you

have no time to do more you can hoist the sail again and leave the luff to a more convenient opportunity—except of course in the case of a lug-sail when you have to haul the tack down to peak the yard. In a loose-footed sail the points only serve to take the weight of the foot and to prevent it from sagging down and getting full of water; there are generally twice as many as are wanted, so you need only tie up alternate ones. In a sail laced to the boom there is some strain on the points. If you can get at them safely it is best not to tie them till after the sail is set again, so as to get the strain even. They should be tied under the foot of the sail, not round the boom.

There is more danger of tearing the sail when turning out a reef. Only the most unthinking man could neglect to secure the cringles before he tied the points, but a moderately careless one could overlook a point, and leave it tied when he cast off the cringle lashing. The only good thing to be said for a continuous lacing instead of points is that you couldn't leave a single turn of that fast, as you could a single point.

Some day you may be caught out in real bad weather, and have to run for a harbour of refuge; and if the harbour is not dead to leeward the procedure for getting there needs care and thought. However much she is reefed down, a boat steers wild with the wind and sea on her quarter; even in the open ocean the wind comes in gusts and the waves in sets higher and steeper than the average, and at such times the only safe thing to do is to take them exactly astern. One has to assume that the weather will get worse before it is better, and that the periods when it will be necessary to run dead before it will become longer and more numerous, so one's first object is to get straight to windward of one's port. It doesn't matter how far to windward; once you are on that line you'll get in somehow, even if you have to blow in under bare poles with a long warp towing astern, so don't lose an inch of offing merely to ease the boat, but shorten sail as required; probably a jib only will give all the speed that is safe. It would be best to have the centreboard right up, and get the crew's weight aft, so that the boat will pay off at once when you do have to put the helm up.

When you are squarely opposite your port you have two advantages beside having the wind in the safest quarter; you are taking the shortest course through the inshore belt where the sea is always worse than it is in deep water, and you

need not skirt headlands where there may be dangerous tide-rips. If the entrance
to the harbour is wide and deep, you are all right; the sea will smooth out as you
get in. If it is narrow and deep, the backwash off the heads will make an alarmingly
confused sea, but not breaking nor really dangerous. But if it is a bar harbour one
cannot tell from seaward what the state of the bar is; if the flood tide is running
it is a good risk, but with a strong ebb—perhaps strengthened by a freshet in the
river—even a depth of three or four fathoms may be a mass of breakers. So if you
know that the tide is going to be foul in the channel keep a bit away from it, and
look out for people ashore; there may be someone among them with enough local
knowledge and boat-sense to point out a beach where you would have a chance of
a safe landing and to help you to pull the boat up on it. If there is, he will detach
himself from the crowd so that his signals may be clearly distinguished; so do not
be in too much hurry to run in, but stand off and on to make known your inten-
tions and to give him a chance to separate and make himself recognized. If the
beach is a fairly steep one you will only have to pass through one breaker on your
way to it, not a whole series, as on the bar; and that one will be quite close in, so
that if it swamps the boat it may throw her and you up high and dry, while if you
swamped in the stream you would be carried out to sea. If it comes to saving life
an open beach is a better risk than a bad harbour.

I have laid it down as a general rule that a boat should be handled with as much
way as you can keep on her, except of course when the state of the sea makes
it necessary to slow her down, but special circumstances call for special rules.
When you are going to pick up moorings approach the buoy as slowly as you can
without losing command of the boat, especially if wind and tide are the same
way. Most people approach down wind at a rate of knots, round up head to wind
straight to leeward of the buoy, and hope they have enough way on to reach it. As
a matter of fact you want enough way to run well over it, because the buoy-rope
will be stretched out by the tide, and you will not be able to get the buoy on board
before you are carried back out of reach if you stop dead right over it. It is very difficult to estimate the strength of the wind and tide when you are going the same
way, and so to judge the right spot to start rounding up, so put the boat close on
the wind abreast the buoy and keep it on your lee bow by suiting your speed to
that of the tide, trimming the main sheet or pulling the jib a little to windward,

and you will sidle slowly towards the buoy. Just before you reach it increase your speed, and put your helm down; the boat will run a yard or two over it and give you a chance to go forward and secure it; leave the jib sheet fast and you will not get hit over the head while you are doing so; there will be plenty of time to get the jib down while she is dropping astern on the buoy-rope.

If single-handed you may not be able to go forward to pick up the buoy; if you have to catch it from amidships do not pick it up with any headway over the ground, but come in sideways at it; don't hold on to the buoy, but get forward in the boat as quickly as you can along the lee side, passing the rope through your hands as you go, but not hauling on it till you can catch it forward of the rigging; by that time the boat will be head to wind, and you can make fast. But if you have to pick up moorings often, try this way of doing it. Bend a long hook—sold as a 'mooring hook' in the West Country—to a short painter, and pass it aft outside the rigging to where you can conveniently reach it; hook to the becket on the buoy and keep enough strain on it to prevent the hook dropping off till the boat begins to take stern way, and she will fall back on it. Take in the jib, and get the buoy-rope on board. In the West they don't get the mooring chain on board, but put the hook into the end link of it, a clean and quick job. That is what the hook was intended for, but a hook-rope so often comes in useful that no boat should be without one.

XIV

MOORING AND BEACHING

Pᴇʀᴍᴀɴᴇɴᴛ ʙᴏᴀᴛ ᴍᴏᴏʀɪɴɢs ᴜsᴜᴀʟʟʏ ᴄᴏɴsɪsᴛ of a large stone or concrete block, with a chain attached which should be twice the depth at high water. The buoy is not attached to the chain—it would have to be a large and heavy one to float that—but to a rope which should be at least one and a half times the depth at high water, and more if there is a strong stream, because it is not meant to lift any part of the chain. See that the buoy is so attached that it floats with a strong stiff becket of rope or wire standing up on top, to which you can hang on with a hook-rope, if, as I advise, you carry such a thing.

Boat moorings also include the various devices by which the boat can be kept afloat but can be hauled in to the shore when you want her. The first, the endless whip outhaul, is of a semi-permanent nature (Fig. XIIᴄ). Lay out an anchor with a large block attached to it by a short chain, and reeve through the block a line long enough for both parts to reach a post or ring above high-water mark. Do not splice the ends together, because the line is sure to unlay more or less, and will run into a bunch of kinks at the shore end; you must unbend the knot and take the turns out from time to time, being careful to keep the ends apart so that the two parts do not twist up under water where you can't see them; if the chain is a short and heavy one the block is not likely to spin. I leave one end fairly long at the knot, and put a buoy on it, and make my boat fast to that, and hope that if other people use my outhaul they will use it in the same way. It is a vain hope, generally they hitch their boats on anywhere, or to both parts of the rope, at low water, so that it can't be moved one way or the other. I am regretfully convinced that most people who muck about in boats are fools, so the whip outhaul is not recommended in places where they abound. Another thing that hampers its use is weed, especially the bootlace kind, which gets packed tightly in the block and jams it. The chain should anyway be long enough for the block to be raised to the surface for clearing at any low water, not only at springs.

You do not want to carry all the apparatus for this mooring when you go sailing, in case you have to land for an hour or two. Something much simpler will do, such as the Riverman's Mooring. A grapnel is better than an ordinary anchor for this—indeed it is the best for any boat work, and a four-armed folding grapnel makes just as good stowage when the movable arms are slid down parallel to the fixed ones (Fig. XIIB). Bend your painter, twice the depth at high water, to the grapnel, place the grapnel on the boat's bows, with its crown projecting, and coil the painter on top of the shank, clear for running; then bend a long line to the crown of the grapnel, and coil it down carefully ashore. Push the boat off stern first as hard as you can, and when she will go no further, jerk the grapnel off her bow with a twitch of the shore line, and if it goes down clear and the painter runs out there she is properly anchored. To get her in to the beach you tow the grapnel in, crown first, with the shore line; it comes quite easily if the bottom is clean, or even moderately rocky, but see that the shore line is a strong one if there are weeds, for you may have to drag up a hundredweight of them as well as the grapnel. Now if you stand at the water's edge and shove the boat off by hand you can only push her the length of your arm, and that won't send her far; so if you can't follow her up into the water get a long stick with a forked end which will fit her stem—a common iron boathook may do, or cut a notch in the end of the blade of an oar—and push with that. Some boats won't travel straight stern first, so turn them round and shove off bow first; the grapnel is just as well tipped over the stern, if you make sure the painter is going to follow it over the side.

The Hypotenuse Mooring (Fig. XIIE) is easiest worked off a quay wall or steep bank; it is not practicable where the tide goes in and out a long way on a shelving beach. Let go your anchor with enough scope for the boat's stern just to reach the bank squarely opposite, make a long line fast to her stern, walk along the bank with it as far as you can, and then haul on it well and make it fast; you will have dragged the anchor rope sideways over the bottom, and the boat will be well away from the shore; naturally there must be no snags on the bottom, and the anchor is better bent to a chain than to a rope. If the wind or tide make it undesirable to tie the boat up head and stern, bend the shore rope to the cable just below the water, and hitch a stern painter to it a boat's length in from the cable, so that you will be able to reach it when you haul into the landing-place.

Another mathematical device is the Mediterranean Mooring (Fig. XIID), only suitable for deep water where there is no rise of tide. Anchor three times the depth of water plus the length of the boat away from the bank, and sling a 56-lb. weight to the middle of your cable. Haul your stern in to the bank, and make fast; now haul in the cable all you can, which will straighten it out and lift the weight off the bottom, and make fast. Step ashore, ease up the stern line, and the weight will draw the boat away from the bank, and keep her there. A 56-lb. weight with a ring on the top of it is a very useful thing to have in a boat, even if you don't want it for ballast; you can ride to it if you have to bring up among rocks where you might lose your anchor.

Various ways suggest themselves for tying up a boat across a recess in a rocky shore or the corner of a dock (but ask the dock-master first). As your mooring lines will probably be on the short side and made fast at some height above the boat they must be watched if the tide is falling or if there is much run of sea, or they will come so taut as to break. In some places you can manage a Gully Mooring, in which the lines are left quite slack; it looks impossibly dangerous, but I have done it several times without accident. In a narrow cleft with straight parallel rock walls there will be no wind but probably will be a considerable run of sea; a boat moored there will range backwards and forwards so much that if her lines came taut she would soon break them. Put a line across her amidships, made fast to either gunwale, and secured with plenty of slack to opposite walls of the cleft; the wash off the walls will keep her quite straight in the centre between them. When you re-embark don't touch the mooring lines till someone has got into the boat to fend her off; fit a supplementary line to haul one end of her in, if you can't reach it with a long boathook. If you have to land on a rocky shore in bad weather, to take off a castaway or to save your own life, this is the sort of place to look for. Don't mind if the sea is running right into it, as long as it isn't breaking. There is a reasonable chance of saving a boat in such a place, even if it hasn't a beach at the head of it; I once left my boat tied across one for three hours, when the swell was rising and falling 6 feet in it.

More commonly landings, forced or voluntary, are made on beaches. This is a thing of which I have little personal knowledge; if I had to do my boating in a place where much beach-work was necessary I should study the methods of the local experts before I tried a bad landing alone. However, for the guidance of those who have to land through surf without professional help, instructions are printed in

the *Admiralty Manual of Seamanship* and in various Almanacs and other nautical publications. *In extenso* they would take up half a dozen pages of this book; here are a few of the points most applicable to our needs.

The beach may be so steep, and the water close up to it so deep, that the only row of breakers is that which falls on the beach itself; running in, either under oars or sail, calls for no more care than in the offing. Or the shore may be so shelving that there are several rows of breakers a mile out from dry land, and before reaching the big breakers the seas will be getting hollower and their crests higher, and increasing care will be needed to keep the boat straight before them. Or the beach may be any shape between these; often it is steep at the top and flat below, so that if the sea is only moderate it will not be breaking at high water, though it may be dangerous when the tide is out.

When running through a line of breakers a well-manned boat may contrive to pass the place where the seas break just at the moment when one is not breaking there—a good surf-boat crew can dodge a whole succession of Atlantic rollers— but two men in a small boat cannot hope to do much in this way; their aims must be to let the breaking crest pass them as quickly as possible, and to keep the boat exactly square to it. While she is being carried forward on the steep face of the wave she may have her bows driven under; she may, if she is a short boat, even be turned over end for end; but if she is kept straight she may not. But if she gets off her course she will certainly be thrown broadside on and rolled over. If she is going in bow first, as the crest reaches her stern the surface water will be travelling faster than she is, and a rudder will be useless. A boat large and heavy enough for her inertia to hold her back till the crest has passed may be steered with a long oar over the stern instead of the rudder, but a small boat cannot be steered at all, and can only be held back by the oars; if she has a transom stern, only by turning her head to seaward and making the crew pull to meet the advancing crest and back her towards the shore when it is past.

The Official Instructions refer to ships' boats, which, if rigged at all, have low and easily-handled masts and sails; they run: 'Under all circumstances, unless the beach be quite steep, take down her mast and sails before entering the broken water ... If she has sails only, her sails should be much reduced, a half-lowered foresail or other small headsail being sufficient.' They do not, of course, contemplate a small boat whose mast is not readily lowered; such a combination is not suitable for knockabout cruising which may involve serious beach-work.

Keep the weights amidships, but rather more in the end of the boat which is to seaward. This not only makes straight steering easier, but it makes that end of the boat cut through the wave-crest instead of being thrown up high by it. That the boat will ship some water cannot be helped; better that than capsizing.

Let us suppose that the boat has passed the breakers on a flat shore and touches the ground where the force of the sea is spent. The crew must jump out and hold her straight against the backwash; if there is much water in her one man should try to lift her stern as the next surge reaches it, or it may fill her right up; as she floats they can run her farther on to the beach on the back of the surge, till she can be baled out and lightened and hauled up high and dry.

Select a straight piece of beach, on which the breakers fall squarely, and away from any rocks, which may make a sideways drag in addition to the backwash, and slue the boat round across the next surge.

'On the steep beach ... retain speed right on to the beach, and in the act of landing, whether under oars or sail, turn the boat's bow half round towards the direction from which the surf is running, so that she may be thrown on her broadside up the beach, where abundance of help is usually at hand ...' If the help is not forthcoming, jump out on the lee side and hang on to the mast so as to give her a good list towards the beach; if no mast, jump out on the seaward side, get the loom of an oar or a stretcher under her bilge and hold her up with that; then the next sea will get under her bilge and throw her higher up. If she falls over outwards, or if her stern slips down, it will fill her. On a steep shingle beach, with everything shifting and sliding, you certainly want abundance of help; it would take two men to get even the smallest boat up it.

Having dutifully dealt with conditions of which I have no experience and of which I hope my readers may long remain in ignorance I come to the more everyday problem of getting the boat up the beach and above high-water mark. Unless she is light enough for her crew to lift and carry her, some sort of gear will probably be wanted to move her. She will slide on her own keel over hard shingle or flat stones—she will also slide on loose round pebbles, but so will the feet of her crew, and they will have no power to pull her—but she will stick on sand, and if she has a centreboard it is better to keep her keel off gravel, which may work up through the slot and jam the board in its case. A boat that is going to be much used on beaches should carry two or more skids or rollers; they do not take up much space, and can be made so as to serve as stretchers. Rollers of course make the work easier, but they can only be used on hard smooth shingle; they merely dig into sand, and must have longitudinal timbers laid down for them to roll on. It is easy to lay down some bottom-boards for this, out of reach of the water (it is not good for the oars to use them), but a boat heavy enough to need rollers will still have a good deal of water round her when she can be pulled no farther on her own keel, and it is no easy job to keep the boards and rollers from being washed away before her weight can be got on them. Half-round skids, though making the pull a bit harder, can be used anywhere; their flat sides, four inches wide, will not sink into the softest sand, and very little into mud. If they are always kept in the water when not in use so that they are thoroughly waterlogged they need no greasing to make them slippery, and it is a convenience to load them a little so that they do not float. If the boat will not run freely on the skids, examine her keel at the first opportunity; probably the metal keel-band is defective and there are nails or screws sticking out of it.

If the boat is a heavy one or the footing on the beach is bad she may have to be hauled up with a tackle, or, in places where the local fishing-boats are beached, with a capstan belonging to one of them. Don't hitch it to your painter, which will merely tend to dig her bows in, but to a hole made through her forefront, preferably through the fore end of her keel, to avoid straining the scarf between that and the stem. All boats should have a means of attachment there; it is the place to tow from, as well as to hook on the beach tackle; some have a corresponding hole in the stern too, in case they are beached stern first. Now, if you are using your own tackle, the shore end must be made fast to something; your own anchor buried well up the beach, if there is nothing good already there. The nearest good holding may be a long way from your boat; it will almost certainly be further than the length of your tackle, so you must put something between them. Don't put a piece of rope, unless you can pick up a hard heavy bit of hemp; any rope you are likely to have aboard will stretch so much that the tackle will come two blocks before it has begun to shift the boat. It is worth while to carry a good length of light chain; it is useful as ballast; it stows better than rope, and it is cleaner if you have to anchor in mud or weeds. It need not be so very long, if you use it in this way (Fig. XIIF). Plant a post—an oar or a boathook, or a light iron crowbar, a thing that often comes in handy—directly in the line between the boat and your anchor; it need not be very securely planted. Make fast the chain or tackle as low down as you can to it, and hold the top of it in taut to the anchor—quite a light bit of line will do for that—and you will never pull the post up, nor need the anchorage be as good as if the weight of the boat came directly on it.

If the beach is, like that at Dungeness, so slippery that you can hardly stand up on it, you can no more pull a rope than you can push a heavy boat. Put a bight of rope round your waist, hitched to your anchorage, and you can pull against that, sitting down to it, if more convenient. Another way of getting a pull without using your legs is to grasp the rope at the full extent of your arms and bring your hands together; you get a very powerful pull, though a short one. This method is particularly recommended for dragging a boat through soft mud, where any considerable movement of your body makes you sink down and perhaps sit down in it.

When a boat has been landed sideways on a steep beach she cannot be immediately hauled up it bows first. The first effect of a pull that way would be to make her pivot round on her bilge and her stern would slip back into the water. One man must get a handspike under the aft end of her keel, to hold it up and prevent it from slipping outwards, while the rest lift her bow up the beach; if it is a steep one and she has a low bilge it must be a clear lift, for they will not be able to slide her up a slope of skids. Then bring her stern up level in the same way. If the boat is a light one two men could work her up, lifting the ends alternately, with less trouble than hauling her up with a tackle. It would be a convenience to have a box, block, or some square pieces of ballast, to put under the outer end of the handspike or skid, to save the need for a man to hold it up. A boat which is often hauled up a steep beach with a tackle should have a hole in the aft end of the keel to hook it to, so that she goes up stern first and is ready to be launched bows first.

If a boat is swamped as she reaches a steep beach she must be allowed to fall outwards as the wave recedes, and half the water will run out of her; right her before the next surge comes, and it will lift her to a place of safety. It is not so easy to get the water out of a boat swamped on a flat beach, but the following might be tried if the force of the sea is broken so far out that a man can keep his feet in waist-deep water. Take everything out of the boat and capsize her; with luck you may trap a good deal of air inside her as you do so, and she will float higher and into shallower water. Get one end of her—the stern, if she has a square stern and has not a fixed main-sheet horse on it—aground, push the cork out of the spile-hole—if you have a corkscrew stick it in first so as not to lose the cork—and you will in time be able to lift the bows out of the water. Replace the cork, drop the bows, and you will have trapped a lot more air. Float the boat up as far as she will go, turn her over; she will still be more than half full of water, but if you are far enough up the beach for no more to come in you can empty her with a baler.

It is unlikely that you will want to launch a boat off a beach in conditions which are dangerous either to you or to her, but a very moderate surf makes the operation a difficult one. Ideally you push her off bows first, start rowing before she has lost the impetus, and get up enough speed to take her through the first line of breakers. It would be easy if the crew were sitting with their oars ready while someone else held the boat straight and pushed her off; not so easy if the crew have to do the pushing, scramble aboard, and get their oars out—if they try to push off with the oars the odds are that the boat will turn round and be thrown back sideways on the beach. It is extremely hard for a single man, because as he gets aboard over the stern the bows will rise and catch the wind and be blown round. The problem is to arrange the oars so that they are ready for immediate use without any risk of getting lost or broken. Place them in the rowlocks, loosely secured with lanyards, with their blades trailing aft over the side; they would perhaps be more easily got at if their blades were cocked up forward, but the wind might get under them and lift them out of the rowlocks. If you are using double thole-pins put the lanyard fore-side of the forward one, so that the oar hangs over the side; then when you swing the handle aft the loom will be pressed against the thole-pin, and if lifted smartly will slip over the top of it and drop between the two pins. If the surf is slight and you can pole off the beach use a spare oar or a boathook for this, having the working oars already in the rowlocks, or there will be a loss of precious time in getting them there.

Some pebble beaches are so steep and slippery that a boat will launch herself down them as soon as the stern-fast is let go. Try to time the launch so that she takes the water just as the surge reaches its highest point, and its backwash with her impetus will take her well out into deep water.

If the breakers only extend a very short way from the beach you may have let go an anchor outside them and veered the boat in stern first when landing, but make sure you have enough rope on board to reach the shore. The anchor out there of course makes it easy to launch the boat again, for you can haul out to it and wait to step your mast and make sail, if the wind suits. Haul the rope through a fairlead on the stem, and then you will not have to lean over the bows and invite a ducking.

The most careful of us cannot help being left sometimes by the tide with a stretch of mud between our boat and the water. In estuaries where mudlarking cannot be avoided, boats with flat or smooth round bottoms are commonly used; it is the keel that sticks worst. If you have to drag a keel boat over mud throw her over as much as you can on her bilge; if she is carvel built and has no bilge keels, and you can keep her keel up with skids, she will slide well enough, but a clench-built boat is more sticky. Push her sideways from time to time, to get the lands of the planks out of the grooves they have made and to let the water run under and lubricate them. And see that there is nothing you want to keep clean near the centreboard casing, for the mud is likely to squeeze up through that; as soon as the boat is afloat, work the centreboard up and down several times to clear the slot and the casing.

XV

LOOSE ENDS

THESE THINGS SHOULD BE IN EVERY BOAT at all times: Spare oar, spare rowlock or thole-pins, spare cork or plug for spile-hole, boathook, grapnel and line, baler. If a rowlock is used aft for a steering or sculling oar it may be regarded as the spare; it is best secured to the stern rig by its own lanyard; spares are safer if lashed conspicuously somewhere near their proper place than if loose in a locker. This applies especially to the spare cork; a cork is easily lost and not so easily replaced in these days of patent stoppers. The standard cork is ⅞-inch in diameter; before you accept it as a spare see that the spile-hole is no bigger. If there is room for it under the bottom boards the best place for it is tied to the nearest frame by a lanyard through the limber—the space between the frame and the garboard alongside the hog-stave or top of the keel—if not, lash it tightly to the frame above the rising or the side seat, where its existence can be checked. If you use thole-pins for rowlocks remember that a spare thole makes a better spile than the human thumb does. I have seen a boat swamped through forgetting this. Always carry the materials for stopping small leaks; tingle tacks and tallow. A tingle is a piece of thin sheet lead; canvas will do as well, if there is plenty of tallow under it; even tallow by itself will stop a fair-sized hole, and it is stuff that ought to be aboard anyway.

Besides its obvious function of holding on to things, the boathook makes a better punt-pole than an oar does; you don't push with the handle of your oar if the bottom is muddy, and pushing with the blade is the finest way of breaking it. Neither oar nor boathook will hold a boat on the edge of a mud-bank while you take a moment's rest, if the wind and tide are strong; she will drive over it and it is broken, or away from it and it is lost. That is when you really appreciate the usefulness of the grapnel.

You may want to pull the boat in to a quay or a rock where there is nothing a hook will hold, but if there is an open joint in the masonry or a crack in the rock you are not yet beaten. Shove the head of the boathook into the crack, give the stave a twist, and it jams firmly. The double-hook pattern is the best for this and

for most purposes; it should be made of square rough iron, not round and polished bronze. The spiked boathook has only one use that I can see; you can hold
on to a round pile if you spear it hard enough. The blade of an oar can be jammed
in a crack, like the boathook, but don't jam it in a vertical crack, or something is
sure to drive the boat ahead or astern and the blade will be broken before you can
free it. If the blade is broken don't throw the loom away; rowing with a broken oar
is more effective than paddling with a bottom board; so is rowing with a boathook
or any sort of spar, the blade is not essential. I have seen a set of sea oars with
blades less than two inches wide.

If the loom of an oar breaks it is because it has not been leathered, or the
leather has been cut and not replaced. Look at a new set of galvanized rowlocks. They are probably malleable castings, and show a ridge or seam where
the moulds joined. Smooth them with a file; the bare iron ought to get enough
grease out of the leather to keep it from rusting. When shipping a rowlock
take care that the lanyard has not got caught inside the crutch, or the oar will
cut it.

Good or bad watermanship are specially conspicuous at landing-steps. Practice landing smartly when you are alone, and you will not be voted a nuisance
when there is a crowd waiting to get in. Unless circumstances prevent it, come
alongside with the boat's head up the steps; then you can put your hand on a
step at the height of your shoulder and by pulling or backing with the outside
oar work the stern in opposite a step at a convenient level for passengers to
disembark on. You must now get your boat away from the steps at once, in the
opposite direction to that from which others approach. Have the painter ready
under your hand, and be sure it is long enough to give the boat plenty of scope,
especially if the tide is falling. If there is a crowd, most of the boats will have
too short painters, and their owners will be glad of the chance to push yours
out clear of the jam. If you can, unstep your mast before coming alongside;
in any case before you leave the boat remove everything that projects outside
her or above her gunwale. If another man's painter gets foul of your rowlock
or outboard motor and whips it into the ditch you have only yourself to blame.
There is always plenty of bad manners and lost tempers at such places; do not
add your quota.

It is often difficult to bring a boat alongside a stone slip if the wind is blowing straight up it; especially if there is a bit of sea. You haven't the riser of a step to check the boat on with your hand, and if the stones are particularly smooth and slimy there are probably no rings or bollards in them. A good sharp boathook may find a crack in the paving, or a grapnel thrown on to it at random may hook something; if they hold, go aft in the boat with them at once to keep her stern in and, unless you can see that the grapnel has hooked something good, jump out with the stern painter. If there is a sea, the water surges very violently sideways across the lower end of a slip, so keep away from that, or the boat may be washed half on and half off the edge, and fall over and capsize when the water drops; carry on till the wall becomes so high that the water no longer pours off it. If you want to beach your boat on the slip do it close against the land-side wall, where the water only runs up and down with no sideways sweep; if the slip is open to the sea on both sides, with no wall on it, give it a miss unless you can see plenty of shore help available. When there is no sea you can land at a slip thus: stand up aft and steer the boat alongside with an oar over the stern; when she touches jump ashore with the stern painter to check her.

Boats have been capsized when embarking passengers, even in the calmest weather. Those already aboard lean over helpfully holding on to the steps, while the one embarking steps heavily on the gunwale. (Sometimes, more fortunately, he hesitates, with one foot on and one in the boat, in which case he puts only himself and not the whole crew in the ditch.) People brought up in boats are apt to credit everyone else with boat-sense; it is safer to credit them with no sense at all and infinite clumsiness. Each passenger, as he embarks, should be made to sit down at once in his allotted place, and told not to move, and each arrival told to step into the middle of the boat—but not on to a thwart, unless you are sure of its strength, for you must assume that he will jump or fall heavily on it. I am sure that accidents are due less often to the carelessness of boatmen than to their reluctance to bully their passengers or to leave others waiting when the boat is already loaded to the limit of safety.

If there is much water in a boat she is easily capsized; so when getting aboard to bale her, step well into the middle of her; don't stand on the thwarts, but sit down at once. It is better to get your legs wet than to go swimming in your clothes.

When you come back to your boat you will find her painter tangled up with and buried under half a dozen others. You should have made it fast ashore with a long loop and a bowline (Fig. XIIIA); no one else is likely to have used that knot, so you can identify yours at once and trace its lead, and you can probably pull it clear of the ring or bollard without removing all the others that are on top of it. The long bowline is a most useful device. It often happens that you would like to hang on to the shore after you have got aboard to step your mast or what not, and you can do that if the loop is long enough for you to reach the knot from your boat. When pulling the rope clear pull evenly; if you jerk it the end is apt to fly up, wrap itself round another rope, and jam.

Not more than half a dozen different knots, bends, or hitches are needed in a boat. It is a good plan to use only the minimum number, and always to make them in the same way; then there is the less chance of making them wrong. A bowline is generally used to make a loop on the end of a rope, but you can neither tie nor untie it if the rope is taut. If, for instance, you want to haul a mooring line taut through a ring you must secure it otherwise, and best with a round turn and two half hitches; that is, twice through the ring and then the hitches round the standing part (Fig. XIIIB). Don't omit the round turn, or if a heavy strain comes the hitches will jam. If the strain on the rope is going to be continuous you can make a long loop with a rolling hitch (Fig. XIIIC), a very useful knot seldom used by yachtsmen, though fishermen often use it for their halyards instead of belaying them. Make one half-hitch, and then follow it round with another turn; pull the second turn tight so as to jam it between the first and the working side of the loop, and it will never slip as long as the end is kept up parallel to the standing part of the rope; it is kept there by making another half-hitch on top of the first. This hitch is used with a stopper for holding a rope taut temporarily, or to attach a handy billy, or small tackle, for an extra pull. One half-hitch, with the end seized to the standing part, holds nearly as well; it is often used for making loops on the end of a wire. For a very temporary stopper make one half-hitch and grip the two parts above it together firmly with your hand and they need no seizing—remember this if you fall overboard and some one throws you a rope's end; pass it round your body under your arms, hitch and grip it, and you can be towed into safety still having one arm free.

The knot I call (with no authority for the name[1]) a topsail sheet bend in Fig. XIIIF is less likely to work loose from a flogging sail than the round turn and two half-hitches, and is easier to untie.

A clove hitch (Fig. XIIID) is merely two half-hitches; it is a quick and easy way of making a rope fast to a spar or another rope. It does not jam, but it is not so secure against side-slip as a rolling hitch. If you have to make the middle of a long mooring rope fast to a post the easiest way is to drop a clove hitch over it; you can do that with one hand, if the other is full of parcels (Fig. XIIIH).

To join two ropes, a common or sheet bend is generally used (Fig. XIIIE). If the two are of different thicknesses make two turns with the smaller. If the difference is so great that even that won't hold you must make a bowline in each, or, if the thicker is very stiff, two half-hitches will do there. Note that you cannot untie a sheet bend if there is any strain on it.

A reef knot has no advantages over the sheet bend except for tying reef points or finishing off lashings; if it is made round a bundle of any sort the parts can be pulled together pretty taut while it is being tied, and it can be untied when there is a fair strain on it (Fig. XIIIF).

Those are all the necessary knots. It is customary to use a fisherman's bend on the ring of an anchor; make two round turns in the ring, a half-hitch under both parts, and another half-hitch round the standing part only (Fig. XIIIJ). But for most purposes a bowline would do as well. The stunsail halyard bend mentioned in Chapter XI is rather a vanity; the object is to have as few parts of rope as possible above the spar, so that it hoists close up to the sheave-hole; but the little extra drift required by a round turn and two half-hitches hardly makes a difference. The stunsail halyard bend is begun like the fisherman's bend, but instead of making the second half-hitch the end is tucked back along the spar under the round turn (Fig. XIIIK).

If the stops on the head of your sail are arranged to slide off the yard you can splice an eye on the end of your halyard and slide that on and off instead of bending it with a knot; but you must know how many stops go on before the halyard. Mark the one next below the halyard with a bit of red tape, so that you can't make any mistake in counting them.

---

1   Better 'bowline hitch'.

I have seen jibs hoisted upside down, which looks bad, if it is nothing worse; but it is not so easy to tell when you pull it out of its bag which end is which, unless you remember that the roping of all sails is on the port side.

Because it is so important I make no apology for repeating here that if you want to keep your mainsail in its proper shape you must keep the spar to which the head of it is bent well greased. All parts of the sailing machine do in fact need lubrication, not only the pins of sheaves. The mast is subject to continual friction from gaff and boom jaws, traveller, hoops, or lacing, unless it has a trackway, and that seldom gets as much greasing as it should. Then there is the internal friction of ropes. When you bend a rope the fibres have to slide over each other; if they will not slide easily it is stiff, which not only adds enormously to the labour of hoisting a sail and to the danger of its refusing to come down in a hurry, but makes the rope become weak at the heart before it shows external wear. Ropes should be lubricated through and through. The nicest rope I ever had was a Manilla whale-line of American make, which had some sort of oil worked in during its manufacture; the next nicest was a lightly-tarred hemp into which I had rubbed pounds of tallow under a tropical sun. They were as soft as silk, not at all slippery to handle, and lasted for years. Do not use linseed oil as a lubricant on either spars or ropes, for it soon dries and gets sticky. Tallow, castor oil, or olive oil are recommended; the cheap qualities have rather a smell, but that soon wears off.

Sometimes you want a rope as stiff as you can get it; for instance, as the becket on top of a mooring buoy. You needn't make the becket all of wire; it is quite easy to shove a bit of wire in between the strands of a hemp rope, where it straightens itself out as a heart and has no tendency to come out again, if there are whippings round the rope where its ends are.

One sees a regrettable number of ropes' ends whose whippings are either insecure or missing. As the rope and the twine of the whipping stretch or shrink according to dry and wet, plain spiral turns tend to crawl back and slacken. The easiest way to stop this is to make an American whipping. Leave the end of your twine a couple of inches long, make half a dozen turns over it, and then hold the end down out of the way; make three or four more turns, which you can do by putting bights over the end of the rope, pull them tight, and you will have the second end of the twine coming out in the same place as the first; heave the two well together and knot with a reef knot. Because this is the easiest of the safe whippings it is the one most likely to be made, and so in a practical sense the best; the more elaborate palm-and-needle and West Country whippings need not be described. The American whipping is a good enough finish to a rope; let it be the same to this book.

INDEX

[Roman numerals refer to illustrations]

CONSTRUCTION OF SMALL BOAT

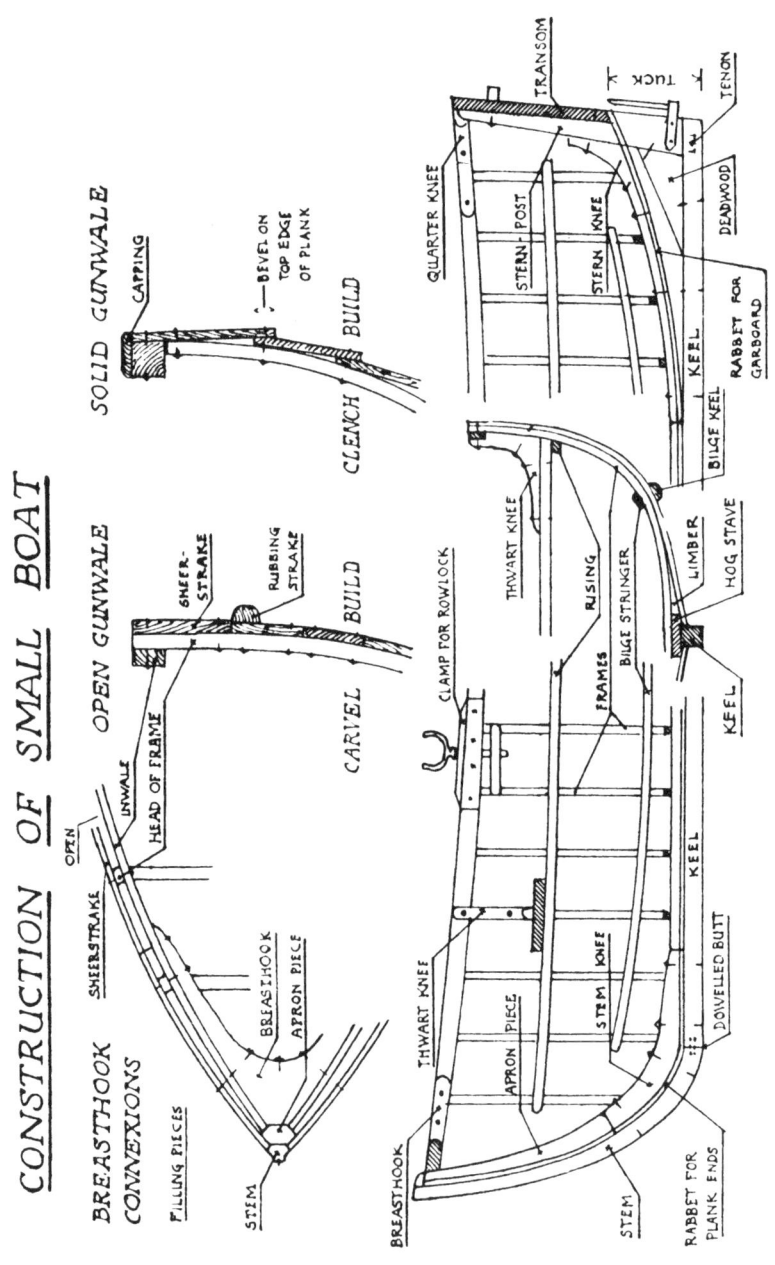

SOLID GUNWALE

CAPPING

BEVEL ON TOP EDGE OF PLANK

CLENCH BUILD

OPEN GUNWALE

SHEER-STRAKE

RUBBING STRAKE

CARVEL BUILD

BREASTHOOK CONNEXIONS

FILLING PIECES

SHEERSTRAKE

OPEN GUNWALE

HEAD OF FRAME

BREASTHOOK

APRON PIECE

STEM

TRANSOM

TUCK

TENON

QUARTER KNEE

STERN-POST

STERN KNEE

DEADWOOD

KEEL

RABBET FOR GARBOARD

BILGE KEEL

THWART KNEE

RISING

BILGE STRINGER

LIMBER

HOG STAVE

KEEL

CLAMP FOR ROWLOCK

FRAMES

THWART KNEE

APRON PIECE

STEM KNEE

KEEL

DOWELLED BUTT

BREASTHOOK

STEM

RABBET FOR PLANK ENDS

Fig. I

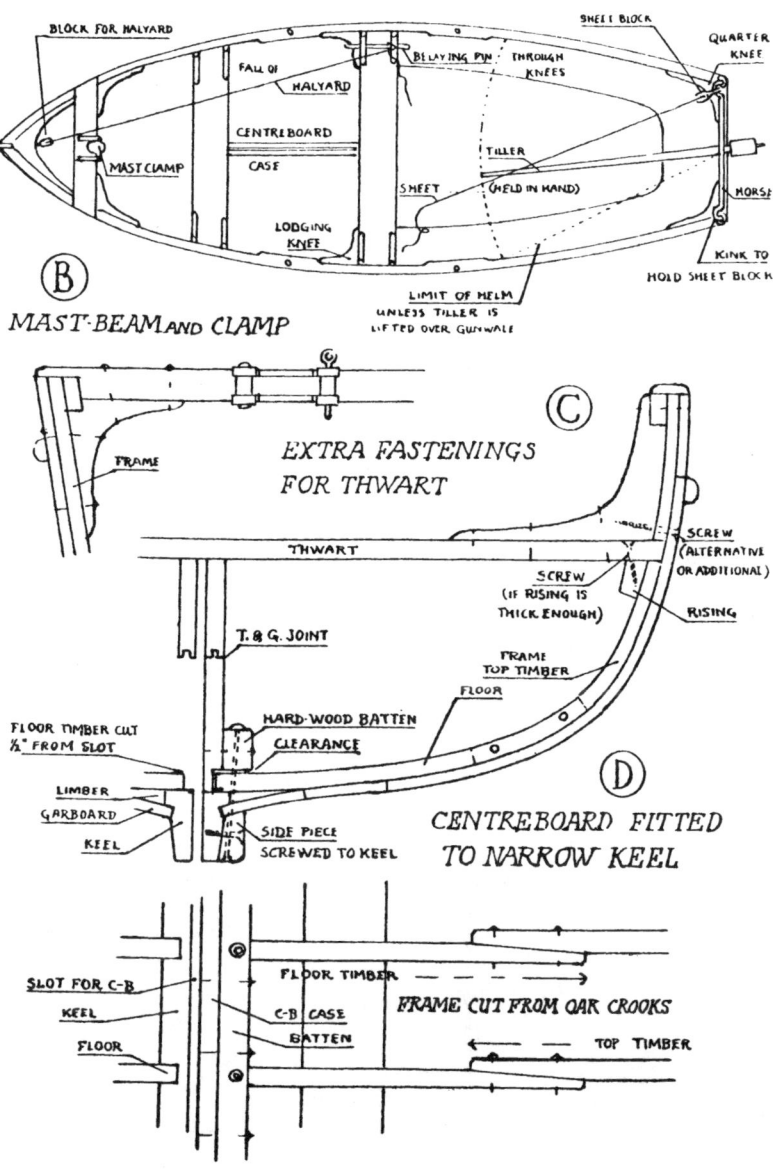

(A) LAY-OUT OF 12-FOOT BOAT

BLOCK FOR HALYARD
SHEET BLOCK
QUARTER KNEE
FALL OF HALYARD
BELAYING PIN
THROUGH KNEES
CENTREBOARD
CASE
MAST CLAMP
TILLER (HELD IN HAND)
SHEET
MORSE
LODGING KNEE
KINK TO HOLD SHEET BLOCK
LIMIT OF HELM UNLESS TILLER IS LIFTED OVER GUNWALE

(B) MAST-BEAM AND CLAMP

FRAME

(C) EXTRA FASTENINGS FOR THWART

THWART

SCREW (ALTERNATIVE OR ADDITIONAL)
SCREW (IF RISING IS THICK ENOUGH)
RISING
FRAME
TOP TIMBER
FLOOR
HARD-WOOD BATTEN
CLEARANCE
T. & G. JOINT
FLOOR TIMBER CUT ½" FROM SLOT
LIMBER
GARBOARD
KEEL
SIDE PIECE SCREWED TO KEEL

(D) CENTREBOARD FITTED TO NARROW KEEL

SLOT FOR C-B
KEEL
FLOOR
FLOOR TIMBER
C-B CASE
BATTEN
FRAME CUT FROM OAR CROOKS
TOP TIMBER

Fig. II

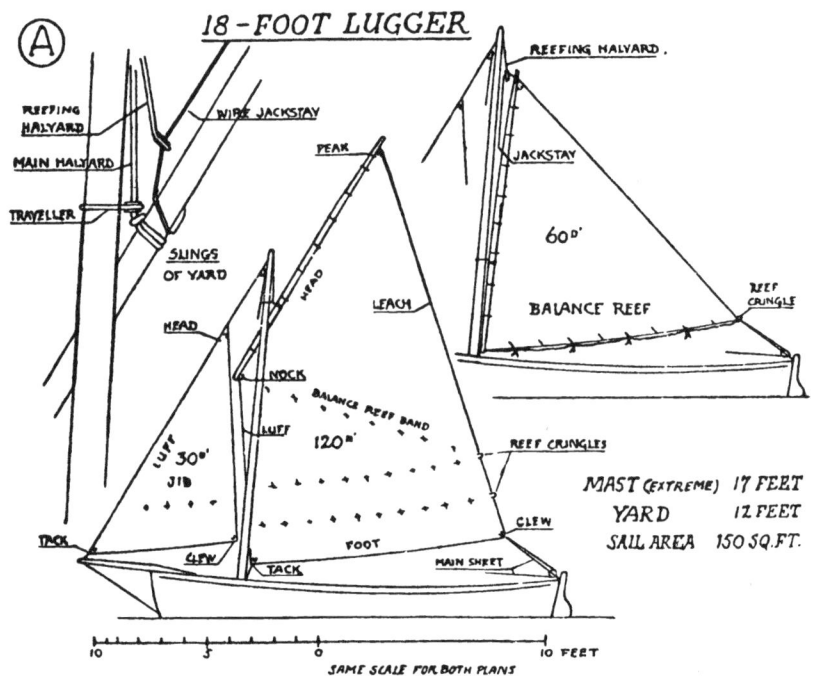

18-FOOT LUGGER

Ⓐ

REEFING HALYARD
WIRE JACKSTAY
MAIN HALYARD
TRAVELLER
SLINGS OF YARD
PEAK
HEAD
LEACH
HEAD
NOCK
LUFF
BALANCE REEF BAND
120°
REEF CRUNGLES
LUFF 30°
JIB
CLEW
CLEW
FOOT
TACK
TACK
MAIN SHEET

REEFING HALYARD.
JACKSTAY
60°
BALANCE REEF
REEF CRUNGLE

MAST (EXTREME)   17 FEET
YARD   12 FEET
SAIL AREA   150 SQ.FT.

10   5   0   10 FEET
SAME SCALE FOR BOTH PLANS

Ⓑ

18-FOOT SPRIT-RIGGED BOAT

HEAD-ROPE
LUFF OF MAINSAIL LACED TO MAST
SPRIT
115°
35°
SNOTTER

MAST   15 FEET
SPRIT   16 FEET
SAIL AREA 150 SQ FT.

Fig. III

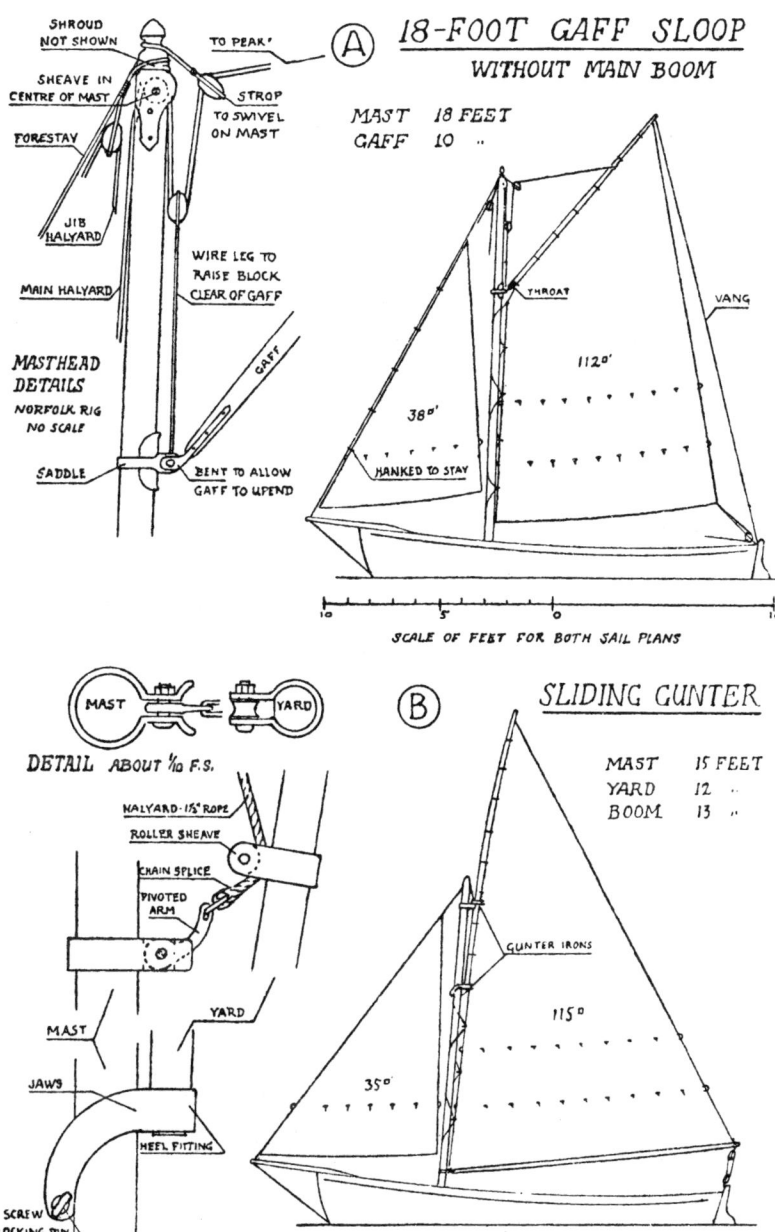

SHROUD
NOT SHOWN

TO PEAK'

Ⓐ 18-FOOT GAFF SLOOP
WITHOUT MAIN BOOM

SHEAVE IN
CENTRE OF MAST

STROP
TO SWIVEL
ON MAST

FORESTAY

MAST   18 FEET
GAFF   10 "

JIB
HALYARD

WIRE LEG TO
RAISE BLOCK
CLEAR OF GAFF

MAIN HALYARD

THROAT

VANG

MASTHEAD
DETAILS
NORFOLK RIG
NO SCALE

GAFF

112°'

38°'

SADDLE

BENT TO ALLOW
GAFF TO UPEND

HANKED TO STAY

SCALE OF FEET FOR BOTH SAIL PLANS

MAST   YARD

Ⓑ SLIDING GUNTER

DETAIL ABOUT ⅟₁₀ F.S.

MAST   15 FEET
YARD   12 "
BOOM   13 "

HALYARD-1½" ROPE

ROLLER SHEAVE

CHAIN SPLICE

PIVOTED
ARM

GUNTER IRONS

115°

MAST

YARD

35°

JAWS

HEEL FITTING

SCREW
LOCKING PIN

Fig. IV

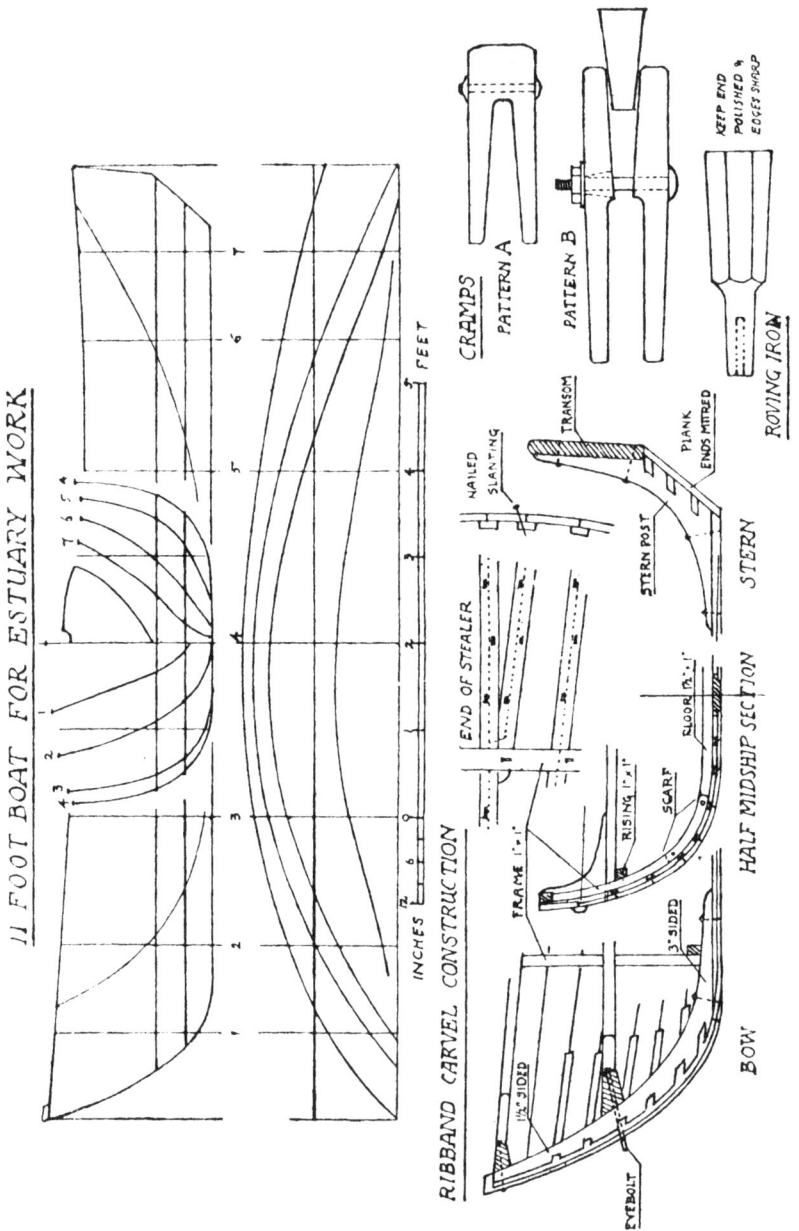

11 FOOT BOAT FOR ESTUARY WORK

FEET

INCHES

CRAMPS

PATTERN A

PATTERN B

KEEP END
POLISHED &
EDGES SHARP

ROVING IRON

RIBBAND CARVEL CONSTRUCTION

END OF STEALER

NAILED
SLANTING

TRANSOM

PLANK
ENDS MITRED

STERN POST

STERN

FRAME 1" 1"

RISING 1" 1"

FLOOR 1" 1"

SCARF

HALF MIDSHIP SECTION

3" SIDED

1½" SIDED

EYEBOLT

BOW

Fig. V

10-FOOT CANVAS CANOE

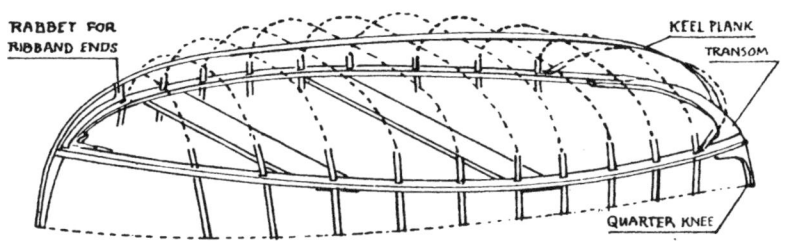

RABBET FOR RIBBAND ENDS

KEEL PLANK

TRANSOM

QUARTER KNEE

ARRANGEMENT OF CLOTHS

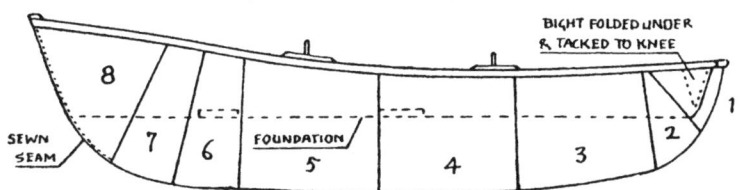

BIGHT FOLDED UNDER & TACKED TO KNEE

8

SEWN SEAM

7   6   FOUNDATION

5   4   3   2   1

DETAILS   NO SCALE

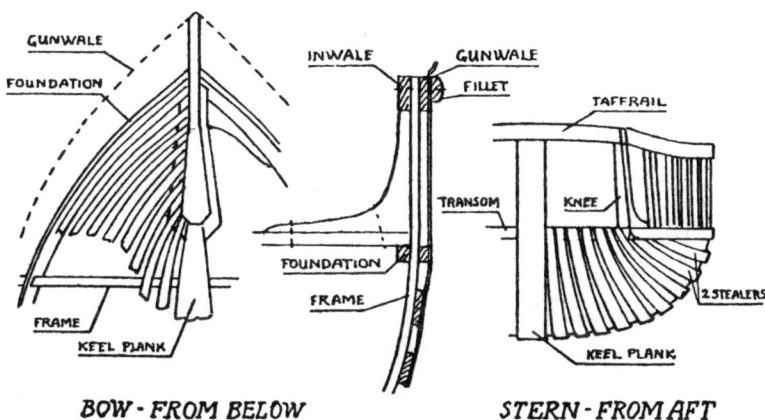

GUNWALE

FOUNDATION

FRAME

KEEL PLANK

BOW - FROM BELOW

INWALE   GUNWALE

FILLET

TRANSOM

FOUNDATION

FRAME

KNEE

TAFFRAIL

2 STEMERS

KEEL PLANK

STERN - FROM AFT

Fig. VI

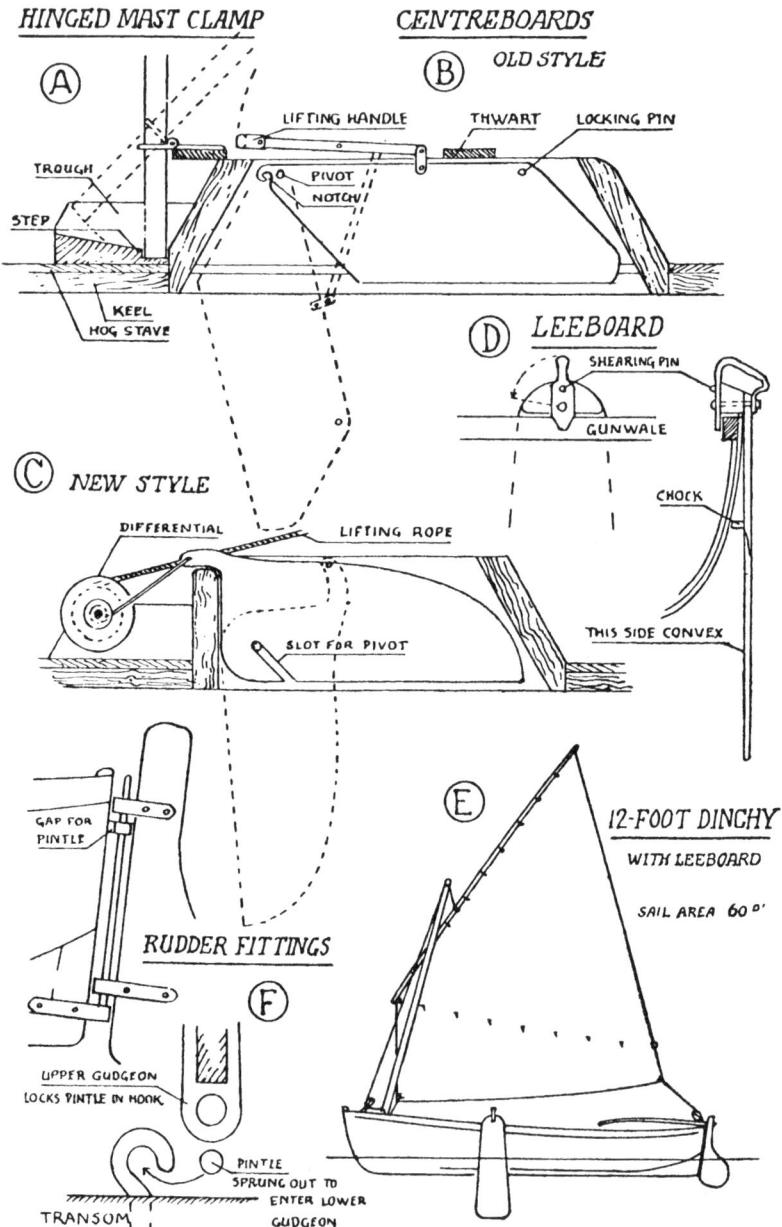

HINGED MAST CLAMP

Ⓐ

TROUGH

STEP

KEEL
HOG STAVE

CENTREBOARDS

Ⓑ OLD STYLE

LIFTING HANDLE   THWART   LOCKING PIN

PIVOT
NOTCH

Ⓓ LEEBOARD

SHEARING PIN

GUNWALE

CHOCK

THIS SIDE CONVEX

Ⓒ NEW STYLE

DIFFERENTIAL   LIFTING ROPE

SLOT FOR PIVOT

GAP FOR
PINTLE

RUDDER FITTINGS

Ⓕ

UPPER GUDGEON
LOCKS PINTLE IN HOOK

PINTLE
SPRUNG OUT TO
ENTER LOWER
GUDGEON

TRANSOM

Ⓔ

12-FOOT DINCHY

WITH LEEBOARD

SAIL AREA 60 □'

Fig. VII

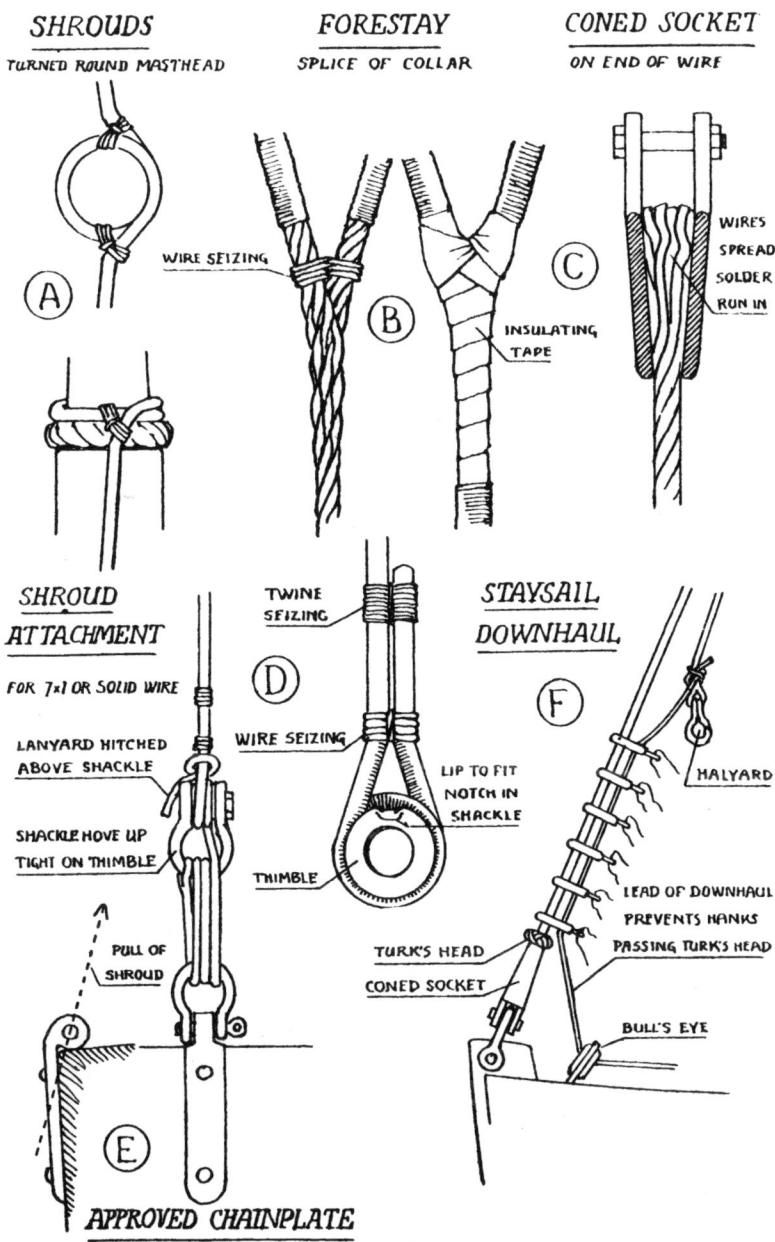

SHROUDS
TURNED ROUND MASTHEAD

FORESTAY
SPLICE OF COLLAR

CONED SOCKET
ON END OF WIRE

WIRE SEIZING

A

B

C

INSULATING
TAPE

WIRES
SPREAD
SOLDER
RUN IN

SHROUD
ATTACHMENT

FOR 7×1 OR SOLID WIRE

LANYARD HITCHED
ABOVE SHACKLE

SHACKLE HOVE UP
TIGHT ON THIMBLE

PULL OF
SHROUD

E

APPROVED CHAINPLATE

TWINE
SEIZING

D

WIRE SEIZING

LIP TO FIT
NOTCH IN
SHACKLE

THIMBLE

STAYSAIL
DOWNHAUL

F

HALYARD

LEAD OF DOWNHAUL
PREVENTS HANKS
PASSING TURK'S HEAD

TURK'S HEAD

CONED SOCKET

BULL'S EYE

Fig. VIII

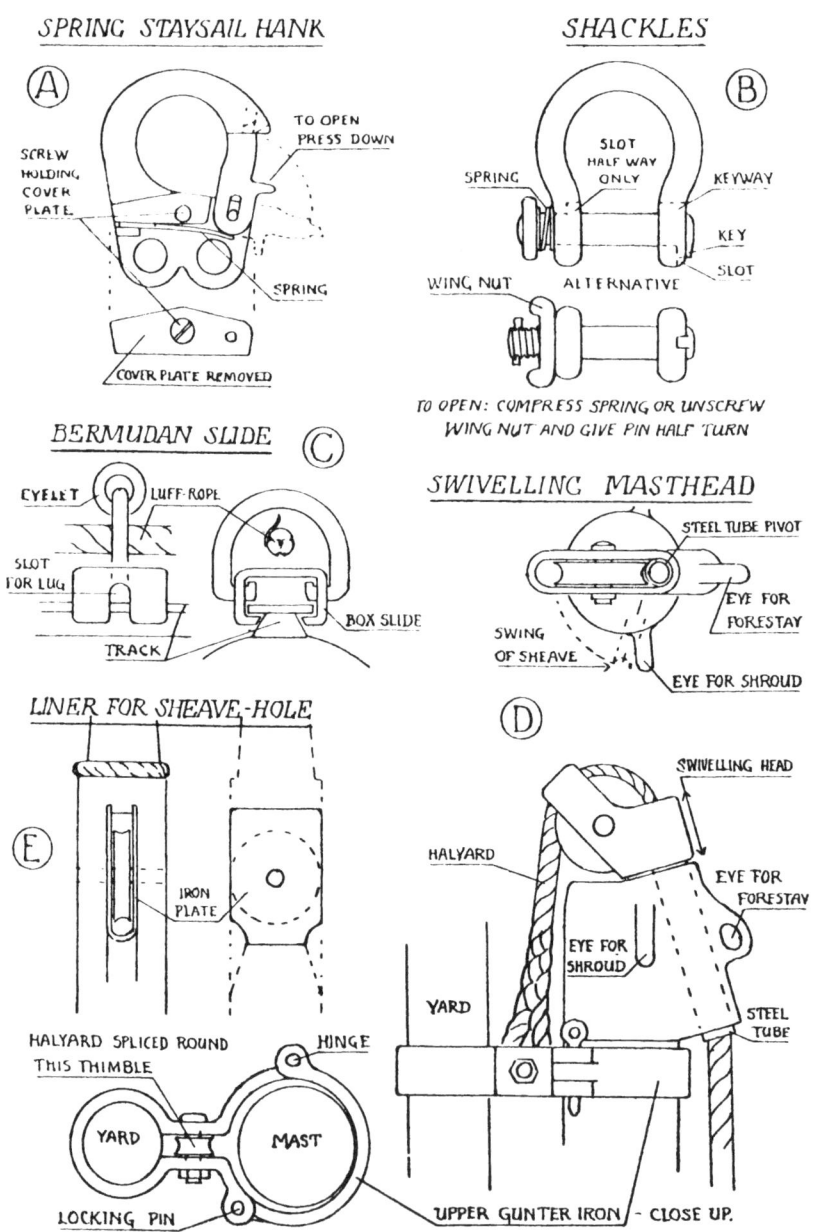

SPRING STAYSAIL HANK

(A)

SCREW
HOLDING
COVER
PLATE

TO OPEN
PRESS DOWN

SPRING

COVER PLATE REMOVED

SHACKLES

(B)

SPRING

SLOT
HALF WAY
ONLY

KEYWAY

KEY

SLOT

WING NUT   ALTERNATIVE

TO OPEN: COMPRESS SPRING OR UNSCREW
WING NUT AND GIVE PIN HALF TURN

BERMUDAN SLIDE   (C)

CYELET   LUFF-ROPE

SLOT
FOR LUG

TRACK

BOX SLIDE

SWIVELLING MASTHEAD

STEEL TUBE PIVOT

EYE FOR
FORESTAY

SWING
OF SHEAVE

EYE FOR SHROUD

LINER FOR SHEAVE-HOLE

(E)

IRON
PLATE

(D)

SWIVELLING HEAD

HALYARD

EYE FOR
FORESTAY

EYE FOR
SHROUD

YARD

STEEL
TUBE

HALYARD SPLICED ROUND
THIS THIMBLE   HINGE

YARD   MAST

LOCKING PIN

UPPER GUNTER IRON - CLOSE UP.

Fig. IX

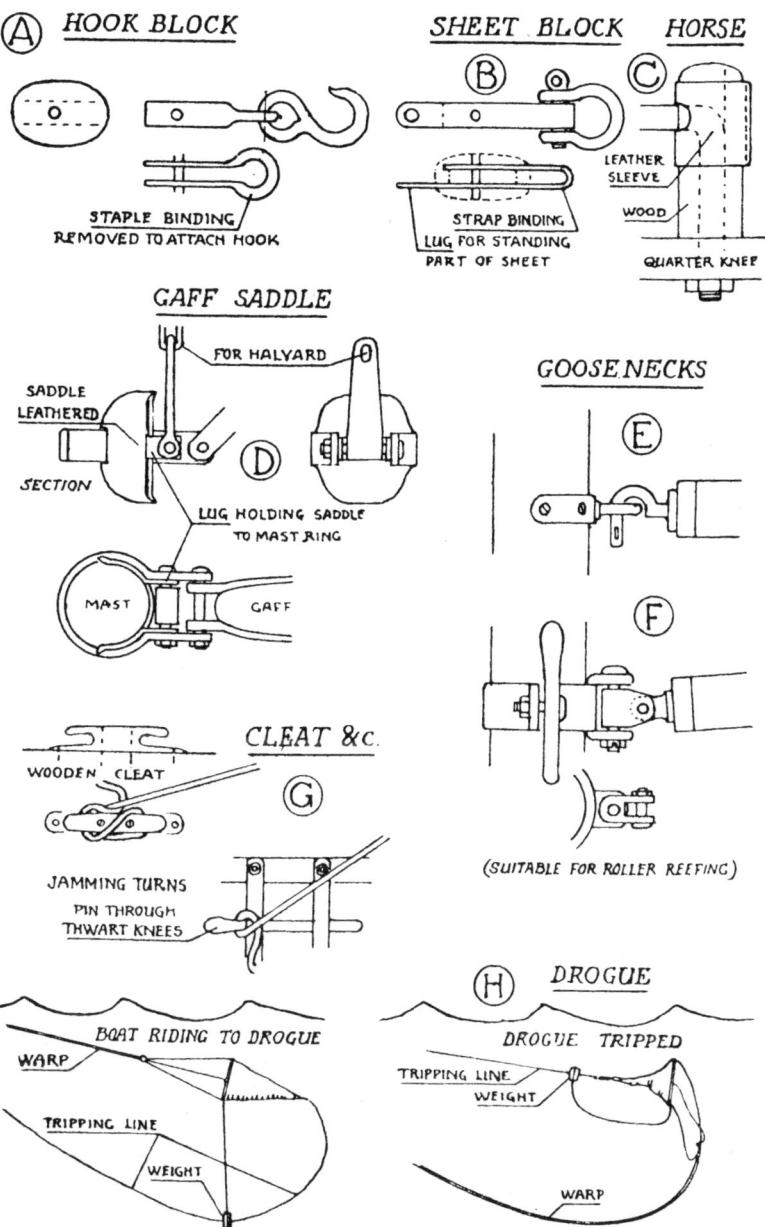

(A) HOOK BLOCK

STAPLE BINDING
REMOVED TO ATTACH HOOK

(B) SHEET BLOCK   HORSE

STRAP BINDING
LUG FOR STANDING
PART OF SHEET

(C) LEATHER
SLEEVE

WOOD

QUARTER KNEE

GAFF SADDLE

FOR HALYARD

SADDLE
LEATHERED

SECTION

(D)

LUG HOLDING SADDLE
TO MAST RING

MAST   GAFF

GOOSE NECKS

(E)

(F)

(SUITABLE FOR ROLLER REEFING)

CLEAT &c.

WOODEN CLEAT

(G)

JAMMING TURNS
PIN THROUGH
THWART KNEES

(H) DROGUE

BOAT RIDING TO DROGUE

WARP

TRIPPING LINE

WEIGHT

DROGUE TRIPPED

TRIPPING LINE
WEIGHT

WARP

Fig. X

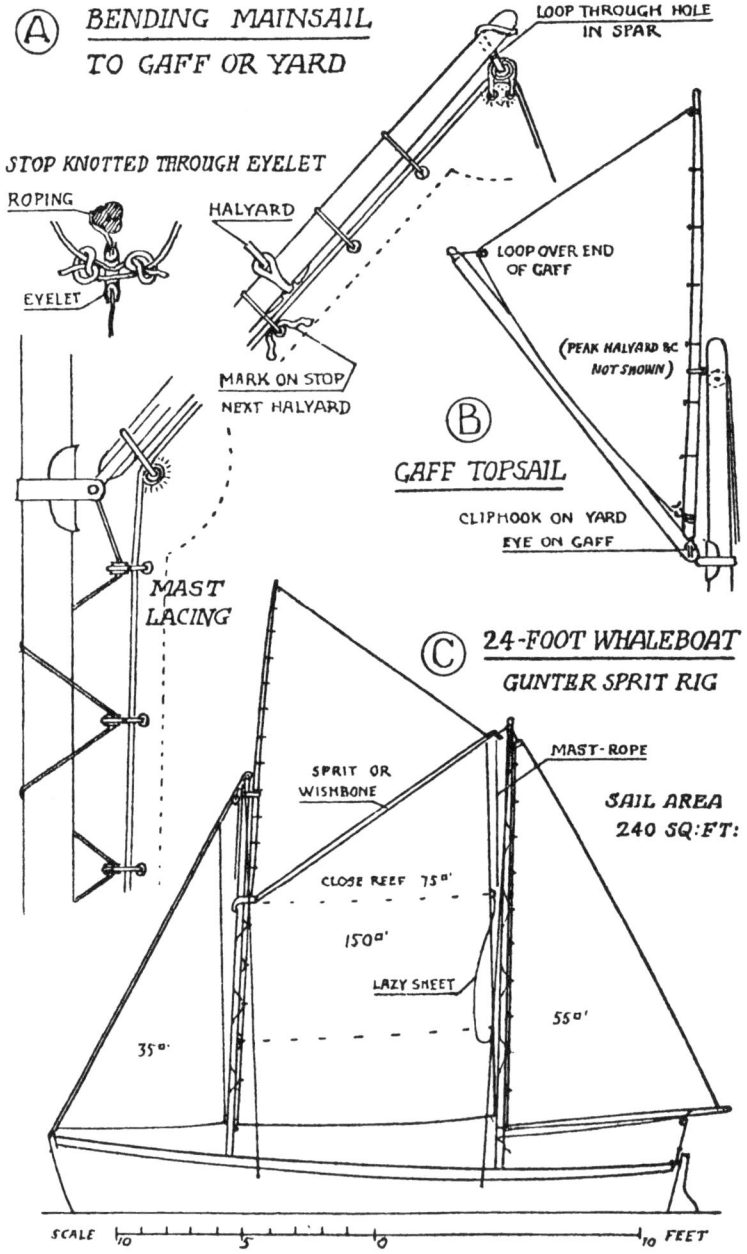

(A) **BENDING MAINSAIL TO GAFF OR YARD**

STOP KNOTTED THROUGH EYELET

ROPING

HALYARD

EYELET

MARK ON STOP NEXT HALYARD

MAST LACING

LOOP THROUGH HOLE IN SPAR

LOOP OVER END OF GAFF

(PEAK HALYARD &C NOT SHOWN)

(B) **GAFF TOPSAIL**

CLIPHOOK ON YARD
EYE ON GAFF

(C) **24-FOOT WHALEBOAT GUNTER SPRIT RIG**

MAST-ROPE

SAIL AREA 240 SQ:FT:

SPRIT OR WISHBONE

CLOSE REEF 75□'

150□'

LAZY SHEET

55□'

35□'

SCALE 10 ... 5 ... 0 ... 10 FEET

Fig. XI

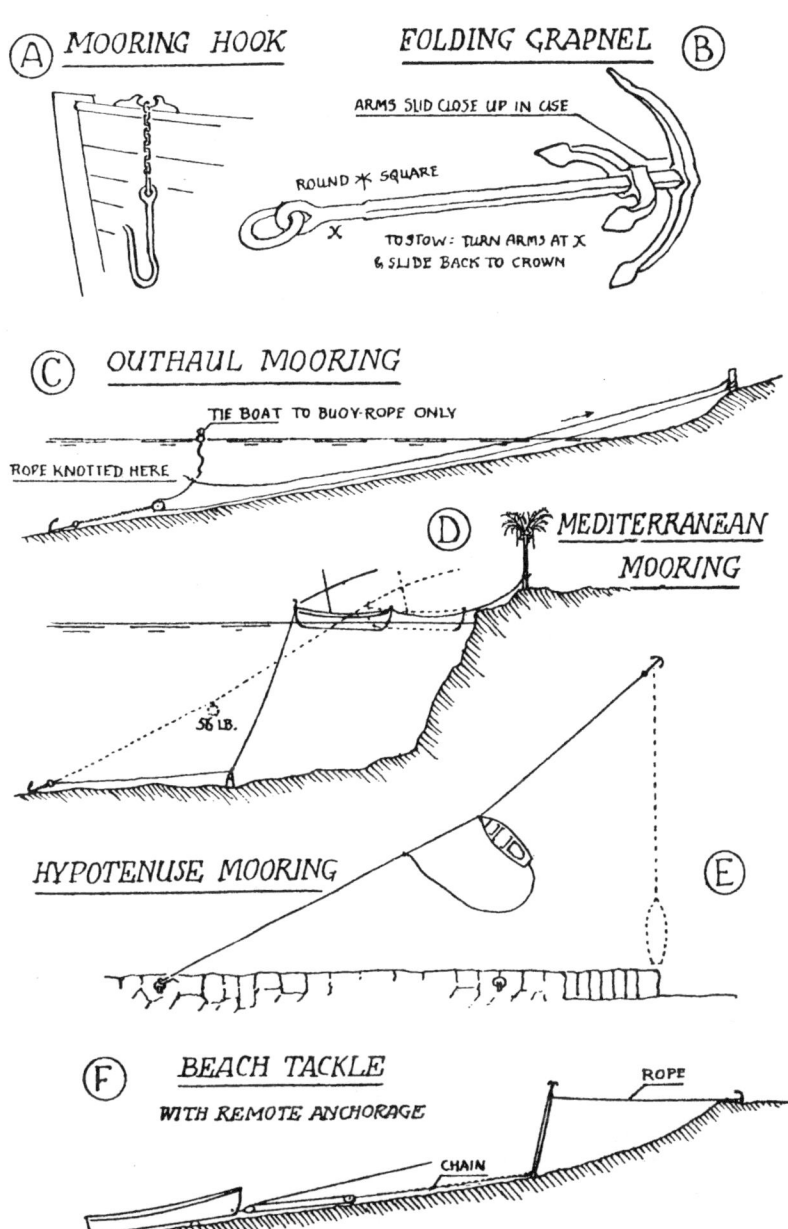

A MOORING HOOK

B FOLDING GRAPNEL

ARMS SLID CLOSE UP IN CASE

ROUND ✳ SQUARE

TO STOW: TURN ARMS AT X
& SLIDE BACK TO CROWN

X

C OUTHAUL MOORING

TIE BOAT TO BUOY-ROPE ONLY

ROPE KNOTTED HERE

D MEDITERRANEAN MOORING

56 LB.

HYPOTENUSE MOORING

E

F BEACH TACKLE
WITH REMOTE ANCHORAGE

ROPE

CHAIN

Fig. XII

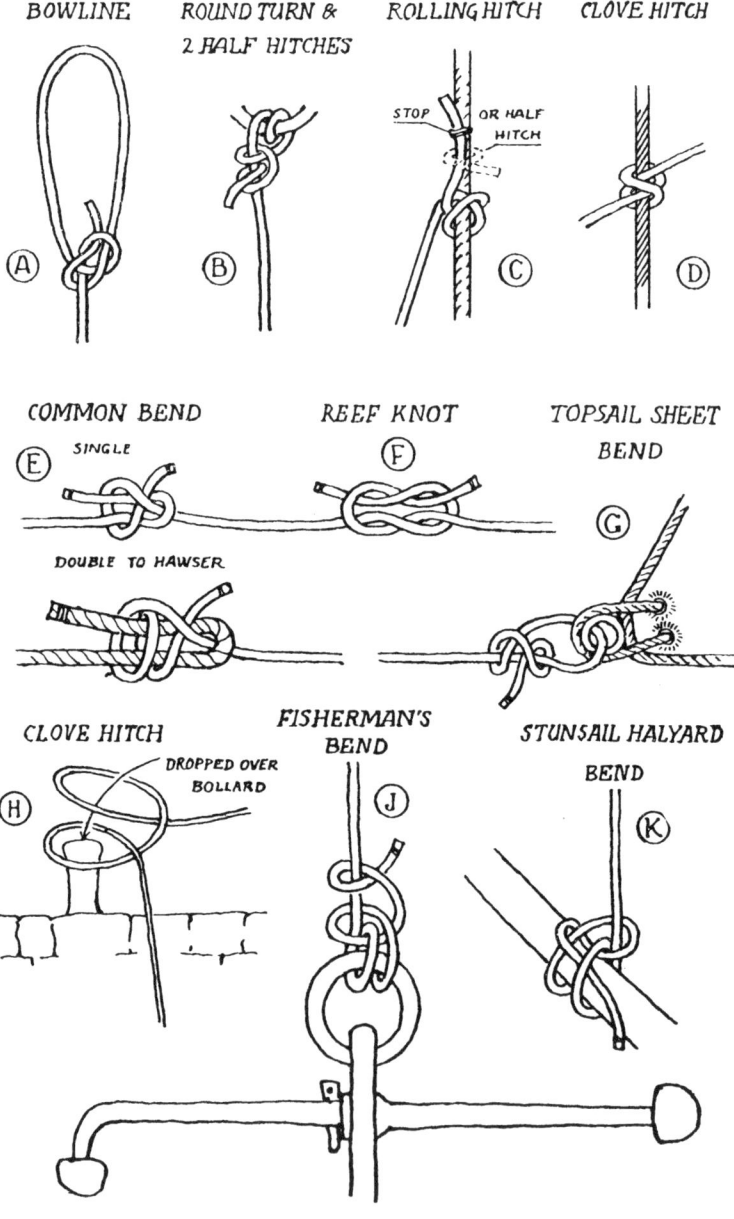

Fig. XIII

POSTSCRIPT

A Small Lugger for the Twenty-first Century

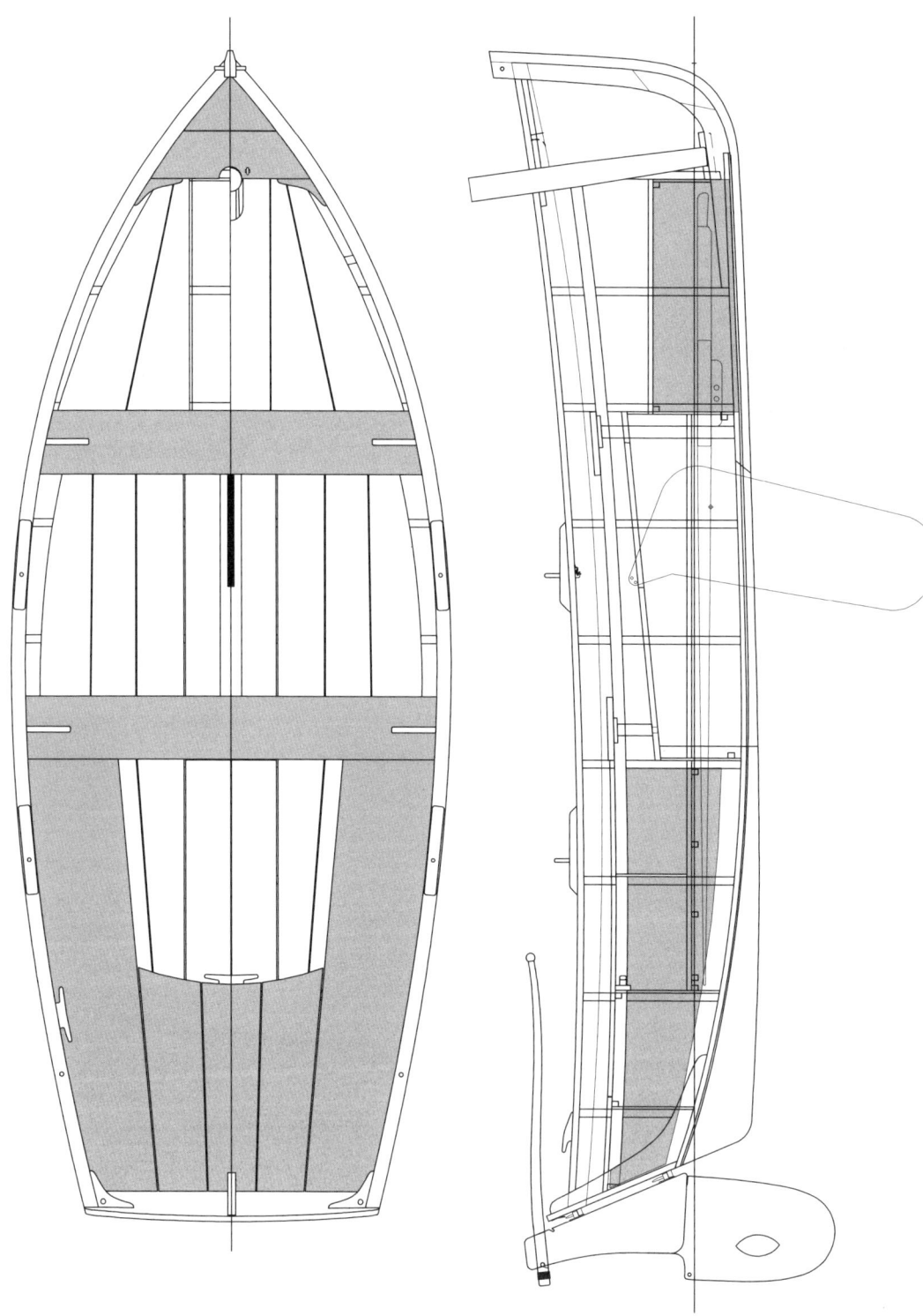

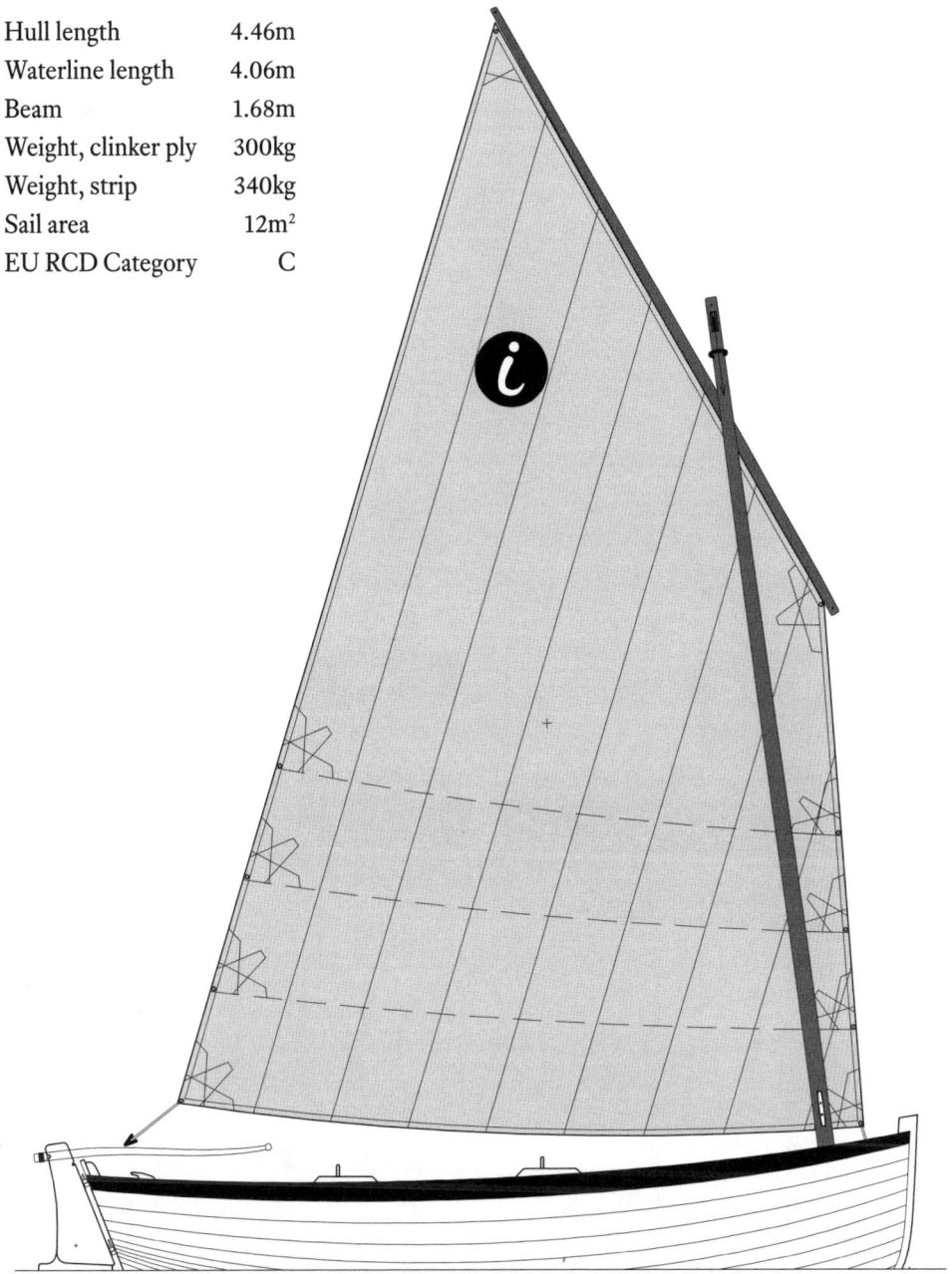

Hull length	4.46m
Waterline length	4.06m
Beam	1.68m
Weight, clinker ply	300kg
Weight, strip	340kg
Sail area	12m²
EU RCD Category	C

ILUR by François Vivier

This small lugger inspired by Breton fishing craft is designed for clinker ply, traditional clinker or strip plank construction, and embodies similar sea-keeping
ability, rig and design details to those advanced by the author in this book. Some
hundreds have been built. Plans and kits are available at vivierboats.com.